D0774997

Simple Architectures for Complex Enterprises

Roger Sessions

PUBLISHED BY
Microsoft Press
A Division of Microsoft Corporation
One Microsoft Way
Redmond, Washington 98052-6399

Library of Congress Control Number: 2008923658

Printed and bound in the United States of America.

1 2 3 4 5 6 7 8 9   QWT   3 2 1 0 9 8

Distributed in Canada by H.B. Fenn and Company Ltd.

A CIP catalogue record for this book is available from the British Library.

Microsoft Press books are available through booksellers and distributors worldwide. For further information about international editions, contact your local Microsoft Corporation office or contact Microsoft Press International directly at fax (425) 936-7329. Visit our Web site at www.microsoft.com/mspress. Send comments to mspinput@microsoft.com.

Microsoft, Microsoft Press, PowerPoint, and Visual Basic are either registered trademarks or trademarks of Microsoft Corporation in the United States and/or other countries. Other product and company names mentioned herein may be the trademarks of their respective owners.

The example companies, organizations, products, domain names, e-mail addresses, logos, people, places, and events depicted herein are fictitious. No association with any real company, organization, product, domain name, e-mail address, logo, person, place, or event is intended or should be inferred.

This book expresses the author's views and opinions. The information contained in this book is provided without any express, statutory, or implied warranties. Neither the authors, Microsoft Corporation, nor its resellers, or distributors will be held liable for any damages caused or alleged to be caused either directly or indirectly by this book.

Acquisitions Editor: Ben Ryan
Developmental Editor: Devon Musgrave
Project Editor: Lynn Finnel
Editorial Production: Interactive Composition Corporation
Cover Illustration: John Hersey

Body Part No. X14-71550

'Tis the gift to be simple, 'tis the gift to be free,
'tis the gift to come down where we ought to be...

—Shaker hymn

Everything should be made as simple as possible, but not simpler.

—Albert Einstein

Contents at a Glance

Table of Contents

What do you think of this book? We want to hear from you!

Microsoft is interested in hearing your feedback so we can continually improve our books and learning resources for you. To participate in a brief online survey, please visit:

www.microsoft.com/learning/booksurvey

Part II The Quest for Simplification

What do you think of this book? We want to hear from you!

Microsoft is interested in hearing your feedback so we can continually improve our books and learning resources for you. To participate in a brief online survey, please visit:

www.microsoft.com/learning/booksurvey

Acknowledgments

This book has benefited from the help of a large number of people, ranging from reviewers to photographers to production staff.

First and foremost is Beverly Bammel. Beverly is the President of ObjectWatch and has worked closely with me on developing the ideas of complexity management and on the production of this book.

Early drafts of this work have greatly benefited from reviewer feedback. My primary reviewers include

- Paulo Rocha, Manager of Enterprise Architecture for Fronde Systems Group, LTD of New Zealand
- Darko Bohinc, Principal Consultant, Strategy Services, Fronde Systems Group LTD of New Zealand
- Dan Schwartz of EDS
- Matt Peloquin, Chief Technology Officer at Construx

It has been delightful working with Microsoft Press. I especially thank Ben Ryan (my product planner), Lynn Finnel and Devon Musgrave (my editors), and Roger LeBlanc (my copy editor).

A number of photographers have graciously allowed me to reproduce their photos. The photo credits are as follows:

- The photo of the replica of Thoreau's cabin in Chapter 1 is by Laura Raney, my adopted niece, who made a special trip out to Walden's Pond just to get me this photo.
- The photos of the Rubik's Cubes in Chapter 2 are used by permission of Seven Towns Ltd, *www.rubiks.com.*
- The photo of Captain John Boyd in Chapter 2 is used by permission of his daughter, Mary Ellen Boyd, who also reviewed the material relating to Captain Boyd.
- The photos of the cockpits in Chapter 2 are used by permission of Richard and Susie McDonald of MIG Jet Adventures (*www.migjet.com*).
- The photos of the orchids in Chapter 4 are courtesy of Orchids of Wickford, N. Kingston, RI. (*www.wickfordorchids.com*).
- The photo of the Jewelweed in Chapter 4 is courtesy of Bruce Marlin, Red Planet, Inc.

Finally, there are a number of people who have contributed to this book that do not fit into any category

- Rodrigo Estrada of Neoris, for many discussions on the nature of complexity in IT systems

- Kevin Drinkwater, CIO of Mainfreight, for allowing me to recap some of our discussions on complexity

- John DeVadoss and Simon Guest of Microsoft for supporting early work relating to iteration through their sponsorship of several of my white papers

- Al Summers of Wiltshire England for allowing me to use one of our chess games as an example of partitioning

- The baristas of Starbucks in Brenham, Texas for their endless supply of Doppio Espresso Machiatos, one sugar, extra foam, preheat the cup please.

My thanks to all of you.

Legal Notices

ObjectWatch is a registered trademark of ObjectWatch, Inc. Simple Iterative Paritions is a trademark of ObjectWatch, Inc. Some of the methodology discussed in this book is protected by pending patents.

Introduction

It was the best of times, it was the worst of times, it was the age of wisdom, it was the age of foolishness, it was the epoch of belief, it was the epoch of incredulity, it was the season of Light, it was the season of Darkness, it was the spring of hope, it was the winter of despair, we had everything before us, we had nothing before us...

So begins Charles Dickens's *A Tale of Two Cities*. Dickens was writing about London and Paris in 1775. But Dickens could have been writing about the field of enterprise architecture, the science of aligning business needs and IT solutions, as it exists today.

It is the best of times. The goal of enterprise architecture is to maximize the business value delivered by IT investment. For most enterprises, large and small, nonprofit and for-profit, public and private sector, the need to maximize the return on IT investment and help IT work more effectively with the business has never been greater. No wonder interest in enterprise architecture is at an all-time high.

It is the worst of times. Enterprise architecture is supposed to ensure that IT systems deliver business value. Too often, it doesn't. Executives are losing confidence that enterprise architecture can make a real difference to IT. This crisis in confidence spans enterprise size, scope, and type. In October 2007, Gartner predicted that 40 percent of all existing enterprise architecture programs will be shut down by 2010. In their highly influential book, *Enterprise Architecture as Strategy* (Harvard Business School Press, 2006), authors Ross, Weill, and Robertson say that fewer than 5 percent of firms use enterprise architecture effectively. In my studies of enterprise architectures and their implementations, I see a common pattern of costly enterprise architectural efforts followed closely by costly IT failures. No wonder confidence in the ability of enterprise architecture to deliver value is at an all-time low.

Enterprise architecture takes a high-level view of the enterprise, focusing on the relationship between an organization's IT architecture and its business architecture. IT architectures describe IT systems. Business architectures describe business processes. IT systems that do not meet the needs of the business are wasteful. Business processes without good IT support are inefficient. Enterprise architectures describe how these two architectures complement each other, ensuring that IT systems effectively support the business processes of the organization.

Clearly, this is a good idea. And yet, enterprise architecture is failing.

What is going wrong? In my experience, there are three basic problems with existing approaches to enterprise architecture. First, existing approaches are too expensive to execute. Second, they take too much time to complete. Third, there is no way to validate their results. So, we have long, expensive processes to create architectures whose effectiveness can be tested only by building large, expensive implementations. Not only is there no way to evaluate whether a given architecture is good or bad, most enterprise architecture methodologies don't even have a standard criteria for what "good" and "bad" mean.

How do you know whether a typical enterprise architecture is good or bad? Simple. You try to implement it. You build the IT systems that support your business processes. *If you* successfully deliver these IT systems and *if* they meet the needs of the business, then you must have had a good enterprise architecture. If not, you didn't. Better luck next time.

In any other field of science this approach would be considered absurd. Nobody would send a rocket to the moon without first testing the planned trajectory against mathematical models for planetary motion; without first testing the planned fuel levels against models for gravity and thrust. Nobody would think of building a bridge without first testing the architecture against models for stress, load, and fluid flow.

Why do we implement large, expensive enterprise architectures without first testing them against mathematically grounded models for effectiveness? The answer is simple: we don't know how. We lack a mathematical understanding of "good." We lack the models for testing for "good." We lack even a basic definition of what "good" means!

Without such models (and definitions), there is no way to validate an enterprise architecture. There is no way to predict its cost. There is no way to ensure that it will deliver business value. There is no way to know if it will even be deliverable at all. *This* is why the field of enterprise architecture is in so much trouble. *This* is why it is increasingly common to hear of massive IT failures; projects that are over budget, late, poorly aligned to business needs, or all of the above.

I was recently talking about enterprise architecture with two high-level architects in a large, highly respected, public sector IT organization. I asked them how often their IT projects came in on time, on budget, and on the mark. One of the architects looked at the other and said, "On time, on budget, and on the mark. I can't think of a single project that we have ever done that met that criteria. Can you?" The second architect only shook his head sadly. I have had similar conversations with architects, chief information officers (CIOs), and chief technology officers (CTOs) in dozens of organizations.

A recent article in *IEEE Spectrum* included this gloomy assessment:

> *Looking at the total investment in new software projects—both government and corporate—over the last five years, I estimate that project failures have likely cost the U.S. economy at least $25 billion and maybe as much as $75 billion. Of course, that $75 billion doesn't reflect projects that exceed their budgets—which most projects do. Nor does it reflect projects delivered late—which the majority are. It also fails to account for the opportunity costs of having to start over once a project is abandoned or the costs of bug-ridden systems that have to be repeatedly reworked.*[1]

---

[1] "Why Software Fails" in *IEEE Spectrum* (September 2005) by Robert N. Charette.

What do we do about this state of affairs? Do we give up on enterprise architectures, as Gartner predicts so many will do? No. We don't give up on the field. The goals of enterprise architectures are too important. Instead, we figure out how to do enterprise architecture right.

By *right*, I mean five things. First, we define what we mean by a *good* enterprise architecture. Second, we use this definition to build up a mathematical understanding of *good*. Third, we extend this mathematical understanding into a formal model for what a *good* enterprise architecture looks like. Fourth, we create a process for developing a *good* enterprise architecture based on that model. Fifth, we validate our resulting architectures against the model *before* we implement them.

This all starts with a good definition of *good*. So here is my definition. A *good* enterprise architecture is a *simple* enterprise architecture. Of two architectures that generally align business needs and IT capabilities, the better of the two is the simpler of the two. The worst of the two is the one that is more complex.

Now it is important not to confuse the complexity of the problems we are trying to solve with the complexity of the solutions we are trying to create. The problems on the business side are certainly complex. Businesses are struggling to adopt new technologies, deal with increasingly stricter regulatory requirements, and trade in a world that is shrinking rapidly. All of these are complex problems, and only getting more so. On the IT side, too, complexity is also the norm. Software systems are becoming more distributed, more heterogeneous, more connected, more critical to the organizations. All of these are also complex problems, and they, too, are only getting more so.

As both business and software systems become more complex, the relationships between them become harder to keep in alignment. Those working on the two sides become more specialized. They develop their own languages, even their own culture. They have less time to relate to those who do not share their overwhelming concerns. A growing separation develops between the business and the IT organizations.

In most organizations, the chasm between the IT and the business organizations is increasing. This will not be news to most readers. Most are painfully aware of the chasm. Few, if any, understand why this chasm exists. IT blames the business side. The business side blames IT. Distrust becomes widespread. Finger-pointing becomes the norm. The business people are making unreasonable demands on IT, preventing them from getting their increasingly stressful jobs done. The IT people are slowing down the business, impeding sales in an increasingly competitive environment.

But the problem is neither IT nor business. The problem is a more fundamental issue that is common to both IT and business. The real problem is complexity. And complexity is everybody's problem.

So yes, the problems are complex. But complex problems do not *ipso facto* require complex solutions. Au contraire! The basic premise of this book is that simple solutions are the only solutions to complex problems that work. The complex solutions are simply too complex.

The antidote to complexity is simplicity. Replace complexity with simplicity and the battle is three-quarters over. Of course, replacing complexity with simplicity is not necessarily simple. But this book will tell you how to do it.

The first thing you need to do to achieve simplicity is focus on simplicity as a core value. We all discuss the importance of agility, security, performance, and reliability of IT systems as if they are the most important of all requirements. We need to hold simplicity to as high a standard as we hold these other features. We need to understand what makes architectures simple with as much critical reasoning as we use to understand what makes architectures secure, fast, or reliable. In fact, I argue that simplicity is not merely the equal of these other characteristics; it is superior to all of them. It is, in many ways, the ultimate enabler.

Take security, for example. Simple systems that lack security can be made secure. Complex systems that appear to be secure usually aren't. And complex systems that aren't secure are virtually impossible to make either simple or secure.

Consider agility. Simple systems, with their well-defined and minimal interactions, can be put together in new ways that were never considered when these systems were first created. Complex systems can never be used in an agile way. They are simply too complex. And, of course, retrospectively making them simple is almost impossible.

Yet despite the importance of simplicity as a core system requirement, simplicity is almost never considered in architectural planning, development, or reviews. I recently finished a number of speaking engagements. I spoke to more than 100 enterprise architects, CIOs, and CTOs spanning many organizations and countries. In each presentation, I asked if anybody in the audience had ever considered simplicity as a critical architectural feature for any project on which they had participated. Not one person had. Ever.

The quest for simplicity is never over. Even systems that are designed from the beginning with simplicity in mind (rare systems, indeed!) will find themselves under a never-ending attack. A quick tweak for performance here, a quick tweak for interoperability there, and before you know it, a system that was beautifully simple two years ago has deteriorated into a mass of incomprehensibility. This book is not, therefore, just about how to create simple systems, but also how to keep those systems simple.

This book is not for everybody. If your organization's systems are typically on time, on budget, and successful in meeting the business needs, you don't need this book. You are either building systems that are much simpler than those that I am discussing, or you have already found a way of managing complexity. Either way, I congratulate you. You are in a lucky minority.

I recently met one such person, Kevin Drinkwater. Kevin is the CIO of Mainfreight, the largest freight company in New Zealand with more than a half billion U.S. dollars per year in revenue. Kevin is widely recognized for his innovative approach to IT and for the cost effectiveness and agility of his solutions. He literally made front-page news in New Zealand by throwing out a $13 million JD Edwards ERP implementation at a company purchased by Mainfreight and replacing it for $25,000 with a home-grown system almost overnight. He was a ComputerWorld CIO-of-the-year finalist and is a well-known speaker. Kevin is also a trusted advisor to his business units, a position that very few CIOs enjoy.

In a round-table discussion sponsored by Fronde and covered by ComputerWorld New Zealand, Kevin and I traded notes on simplicity in enterprise architectures. As I drew my pictures of an ideal simple architecture and Kevin drew his, we were both struck by their similarities. Kevin does not need me to evangelize simplicity. He and his entire IT organization eat, drink, and breathe simplicity every day. It is the core architectural requirement of everything they do. It is the primary reason that when Kevin delivers an IT solution, that solution is typically on time, on budget, and spot on the mark with regard to the business requirements.

If you are like Kevin, you don't need this book. However, if your organization's systems are typically late and over budget, and you sense a growing rift between the technical and business sides of the organization, your organization *does* need this book. If you are an IT executive, IT manager, software architect, or business analyst involved in a project whose complexity seems to be growing exponentially, you might find this book transformative.

I say this book might be transformative because it just might transform your understanding of enterprise architectures. It might change why you think we want them, how we can create them better, how we can implement them more effectively, and how they can provide greater business value.

It all comes down to simplicity. Simplicity as a core value. Simplicity as an enabler. Simplicity as a business asset. As one chief architect of a major airline recently told me, "I have been talking to many organizations about enterprise architecture. They all tell me the same thing. None of it sticks. You are the first one to discuss enterprise architecture differently. And you are the first one to make any sense." It isn't *me* that makes sense. It is *simplicity*.

How do you make things simple? Simple. Get rid of complexity. Understand it, recognize it, eliminate it, and banish it. By the time you finish this book, you will know how to do this. You will understand the mathematics of complexity, the models that govern complexity, the processes that eliminate complexity, and the validation approach that ensures complexity is no longer haunting your enterprise architectures. Your life and your architectures, then, will be so much simpler.

So while this book is ostensibly about enterprise architecture, it is really about something even more basic: simplicity. The approach to controlling complexity presented in this book can be applied successfully to either business architectures or IT architectures. But this approach is most effective when applied at the level that includes *both* business *and* IT architectures. This is the level of enterprise architecture.

The Organization of This Book

This book starts by giving an intuitive understanding of complexity, moves to a more formal understanding, and then finally moves to a more process-focused discussion. The particular process that I advocate is called SIP, for simple iterative partitions. SIP is the only enterprise architectural methodology that specifically focuses on the problem of complexity.

Part I, "The Question of Complexity," gives a basic understanding of the issue of complexity in enterprise architectures.

Chapter 1, "Enterprise Architecture Today," gives a general introduction to the field of enterprise architecture, including an overview of the major methodologies used today and where they stand on the issue of complexity.

Chapter 2, "A First Look at Complexity," introduces in a nonmathematical way the main concepts of partitioning, iteration, and simplification, and the relationship of these three ideas to complexity control. As you will see in this chapter, you can learn quite a bit about enterprise architectures by looking at executive lunches, emergency rescues, and even chess games!

Chapter 3, "Mathematics of Complexity," gives a formal introduction to the mathematics of complexity. No mathematical background is assumed, so don't worry. We are looking at very simple dice throwing, partitioning, and Boolean math. These concepts, which are all explained from the ground up, are the basis for our model for complexity. This model helps us better understand how complexity changes as we manipulate partitions of our enterprise.

Part II, "The Quest for Simplicity," describes the specific methodology that I advocate to address complexity in enterprise architectures.

Chapter 4, "The ABCs of Enterprise Partitions," introduces the concept of an autonomous business capability (ABC). The ABC is the enterprise equivalent of a partition subset. Understanding the nature of ABCs and how they relate to each other sets the stage for the methodology we will use to create enterprise architectures that embrace simplicity as a core value.

Chapter 5, "SIP Process," describes the methodology of simple iterative partitions (SIP) in detail. This is our methodology for controlling complexity. It is grounded in the mathematics of complexity and is based on identifying, manipulating, repartitioning, and reorganizing ABCs.

Chapter 6, "A Case Study in Complexity," looks at an actual case study of a highly complex project, the National Programme for IT, part of Britain's National Health Care System. If you think you have seen complexity before, just wait. This system has already cost billions of dollars, brought several companies to the brink of financial disaster, and, most likely, will end up with the dubious distinction of being the world's largest IT failure. This chapter discusses what went wrong and how the SIP methodology could have helped save this project.

Chapter 7, "Guarding the Boundaries: Software Fortresses," looks at the software components of ABCs and discusses some of the special challenges they face in maintaining the integrity of the boundaries separating autonomous systems. I'll describes a pattern called *software fortresses* that allows you to apply the simplification algorithms of SIP to software systems.

Chapter 8, "The Path Forward," reviews the main points of this book and describes how you can take your new understanding of complexity and use it to drive a corporate culture that embraces simplicity.

The book then concludes with an appendix, "This Book at a Glance," which gives a concise description of the main mathematical rules, the SIP methodology, and the software fortress model. After this, you will be a bona fide member of the Anti-Complexity League, ready to defend the simplicity of your enterprise architecture against every insidious attack.

Find Additional Content Online

As new or updated material becomes available that complements your book, it will be posted online on the Microsoft Press Online Developer Tools Web site. The type of material you might find includes updates to book content, articles, links to companion content, errata, sample chapters, and more. The Web site will be available soon at *http://www.microsoft.com/ learning/books/online/developer*, and will be updated periodically.

Support for This Book

Microsoft Press provides support for books and companion content at the following Web site: *http://www.microsoft.com/learning/support/books/*.

Questions and Comments

If you have comments, questions, or ideas regarding the book or the companion content, or if you have questions that are not answered by visiting the sites previously listed, please send them to Microsoft Press via e-mail to

mspinput@microsoft.com

Or via postal mail to

Microsoft Press
Attn: *Simple Architectures for Complex Enterprises* Editor
One Microsoft Way
Redmond, WA 98052-6399

Please note that Microsoft software product support is not offered through the above addresses.

Part I
The Question of Complexity

Chapter 1
Enterprise Architecture Today

This book is about how to do enterprise architecture better. This immediately brings up the question, better than what? Better than we do things today. I will address issues that I think are important that are not addressed by today's methodologies. The most important of these issues is, of course, complexity.

But before I can discuss how I think things need to be improved, you need to understand the current state of the art. What are the methodologies that I think need improvements? How do these methodologies address complexity, if at all?

Most enterprise architects have some experience with one of these methodologies, but few enterprise architects have a broad perspective on the field. In this chapter, I will give some background about the field of enterprise architecture. I will discuss why the field exists and what the field looks like today. I will compare the major enterprise architecture methodologies in use and their relationship to each other.

Each of these methodologies has important contributions to make to the practicing enterprise architect's tool chest. And although most people treat these methodologies as mutually exclusive (you can use Zachman, TOGAF, or FEA), in reality they are complementary and you should have an awareness of what each can contribute to solving the problems at hand.

But just as you should be aware of what each of these methodologies can contribute, you should also be aware of what each lacks. None of these methodologies provides a complete solution to creating an enterprise architecture. Even all of them combined do not offer a complete solution. This is my reason for writing this book: to fill in the missing piece.

The missing piece is a way to manage complexity. These methodologies can help you understand your business processes and how to better serve those processes with technology. But they can only do so effectively if you have first brought some order to the enterprise. This book will show you how to tame your enterprise to the point where these methodologies can be brought into play effectively.

So this chapter is really about the current state of the art of enterprise architecture. What works, what doesn't work, and what is needed to complete the picture.

Why Bother?

Creating an enterprise architecture is a significant undertaking for an organization, requiring time, resources, and cultural change. Why should an organization bother?

I'll go through some of what are, in my experience, typical concerns that lead enterprises to consider creating an enterprise architecture and how a successful enterprise architecture can deliver value by addressing those concerns. If one or more of these enterprise concerns seems applicable to your organization, you are a good candidate to consider implementing an enterprise architecture. If not, consider yourself lucky.

Issue: Unreliable Enterprise Information

Enterprises are dependent on reliable information about their operations to make good business decisions. An enterprise that either cannot access or trust its information will, at best, be constantly second-guessing its decisions and, at worst, make decisions based on inaccurate information. Either is a serious problem.

Unreliable information is frequently a result of data duplication across multiple information technology (IT) systems that span multiple uncoordinated business processes.

An enterprise architecture can help an organization understand what information is unreliable, how it affects the organization, and what steps are necessary to solve the problem.

Issue: Untimely Enterprise Information

Enterprises are dependent on not only reliable information (as previously mentioned) but on information being presented in a timely fashion. Enterprises need timely information to make agile business decisions. Enterprises that do not have access to timely information end up making business decisions based on stale information, which is like playing chess without being allowed to know your opponent's last move. These enterprises will find it difficult to compete against enterprises that are making decisions based on what is happening now.

Untimely information is frequently a result of highly human-driven operations. Human-driven operations is a sign that IT is not well aligned with the business needs.

An enterprise architecture can help an organization understand how to better use technology and reduce the dependencies on human operations.

Issue: New Complex Projects Underway

Enterprises that are preparing to undertake highly complex IT projects are often concerned about managing that complexity and, if they are not concerned, they should be. Building a new, highly complex IT project without fully understanding its relationship to the business processes is unlikely to be successful.

An enterprise architecture can be critical to helping the IT department understand exactly what the business needs are before it begins a new project, greatly increasing the odds that the project will be successful.

Issue: New Companies Being Acquired

When one company acquires another, it can be very difficult to merge the two sets of business processes and IT systems.

An enterprise architecture for both organizations can be a great help in seeing how the business processes and IT systems complement each other and how they can be merged together.

Issue: Enterprise Wants to Spin Off Unit

Sometimes a company wants to sell off some unit of the business. The value of any business unit is greatly increased if it is autonomous from the rest of the business and easily integrated into another organization's operations. That autonomy also helps ensure that the enterprise that remains is minimally affected by the spinoff.

An enterprise architecture can help an organization understand the impact on the business processes and IT systems of the spinoff.

Issue: Need to Identify Outsourcing Opportunities

Frequently, enterprises decide to focus on their core strengths and outsource support functions. This business strategy requires an understanding of how the core IT systems and business processes relate to the support IT systems and business processes.

An enterprise architecture can help an organization understand where the opportunities for outsourcing exist, and how it can be accomplished with minimal disruption of operations.

Issue: Regulatory Requirements

Governments around the world are taking a hard line on how enterprises manage their information. Privacy regulations require companies to prove that only authorized individuals can access various types of information. Auditing regulations require that organizations can trace back data changes to specific business process events. Many enterprises are faced with trying to meet these regulations with highly convoluted software systems wherein data is randomly shared in often unexpected and undocumented patterns.

An enterprise architecture can help business managers understand the data usage patterns and how those patterns relate to business functions.

Issue: Need to Automate Relationships with External Partners

The clear trend in the business world is to automate relationships between partners. The line between retailers and suppliers is becoming increasingly blurred, with suppliers sometimes having access to inventory information in ways that would have been unthinkable a decade ago. Much of this automation makes use of industry-standard Web services for passing messages between partners.

Enterprises that seek to participate in these relationships need to have well-defined business processes that are closely aligned with their IT systems.

An enterprise architecture can help define those business processes and pinpoint opportunities for automation.

Issue: Need to Automate Relationships with Customers

Today's customers expect online access to search for merchandise, place orders, check the status of orders, and look for product support information. From the customer perspective, such capability is convenient. From the business perspective, such capability is highly cost-effective. This is a win-win situation.

An enterprise architecture can help determine how customers can access business systems without compromising necessary protection of data and protected business functions.

Issue: Poor Relationship Between IT and Business Units

In many enterprises, we can see the alarming trend of creating a separation between IT groups and business groups. I discussed this problem in the Preface. The IT group sees the business groups as unreasonable. The business groups see the IT group as unable to deliver the desired functionality. The IT group does more and more without consulting the business groups. The business groups try more and more to circumvent IT. Distrust between the groups becomes normal and even expected. Clearly, this is an unhealthy situation for an organization.

An enterprise architecture can provide a neutral watering hole at which both the business and IT groups can meet and discuss how best to work together.

Issue: Poor Interoperability of IT Systems

Many enterprises have a large and rapidly evolving collection of IT systems that were developed and/or acquired independently and built on incompatible platforms. The IT group is left with the challenge of getting these systems to coordinate their work and share information. Frequently, these systems are glued together in a patchwork fashion. Often the juncture points are poorly documented, highly fragile, and unreliable. The result is systems that are tied together in random ways, with failures in one system propagating in unpredictable ways to other systems. The IT backbone of an enterprise is only as strong as its weakest link. For far too many organizations, there are far too many of these weak links.

An enterprise architecture is critical to understanding how to improve the interoperability of these systems.

Issue: IT Systems Unmanageable

As I mentioned in the last section, IT systems are frequently built up piecemeal and patched together haphazardly. In addition to creating the interoperability problem that I just discussed, this cobbling together of IT systems also often results in what I call *pinned architectures*—that is, architectures in which one system can't easily be changed because any changes could affect other systems in unacceptable and sometimes unpredictable ways. When changes must be made, it becomes very expensive, and very risky, to do so.

An enterprise architecture is the starting point to understanding how IT systems are related to each other.

The Value of Enterprise Architecture

Do any of these issues seem familiar? If so, your organization can probably benefit from creating an enterprise architecture. Are any of these problems your problems? If so, at least part of your job is the role of an enterprise architect, regardless of the title that might be on your business card.

Later, you will see how finding the solutions to these problems can be greatly aided by having a defined approach to managing complexity. But let's start by seeing where most methodologies are today.

Common Definitions

Before I get too far into discussing enterprise architecture, I need to define some terms. These definitions are especially important in comparing methodologies, because different methodologies sometime use similar terms to mean different things.

For example, we have two popular methodologies that describe themselves as *enterprise architectural frameworks*: the Zachman Framework for Enterprise Architectures and The Open Group Architectural Framework (TOGAF). Yet these two methodologies share little in common other than the words *enterprise*, *architecture*, and *framework*. Even using the term *methodology* to describe these two approaches is questionable. As John Zachman himself has reminded me on more than one occasion, his approach is a *classification scheme* for organizing systems, not a *method* for doing anything.

So I will start by defining the terms as I will use them in this book:

- **Architect**   One whose responsibility is the design of an architecture and the creation of an architectural description.

- **Architectural artifact**   A specific document, report, analysis, model, or other tangible item that contributes to an architectural description.

- **Architectural description**   A collection of architectural artifacts that collectively document an architecture.

- **Architectural framework**   A skeletal structure that defines suggested architectural artifacts, describes how those artifacts are related to each other, and provides generic definitions for what those artifacts might look like.

- **Architectural methodology**   A generic term that can describe any structured approach to solving some or all of the problems related to architecture.

- **Architectural process**   A defined series of actions directed to the goal of producing either an architecture or an architectural description.

- **Architectural taxonomy**   A methodology for organizing and categorizing architectural artifacts.

- **Architecture**   The fundamental organization of a system, including how that system is related to its environment and what principles guided its design and evolution.

- **Enterprise architecture**   An architecture in which the system in question is the whole enterprise, especially the business processes, technologies, and information systems of the enterprise.

What Is Enterprise Architecture?

The definition just given of an enterprise architecture is pretty high level. Because enterprise architecture is the topic of this book, let's look at the term in a bit more depth.

According to Carnegie Mellon University (home of some of the thought leaders in this field), an enterprise architecture is defined as follows:

> *A means for describing business structures and processes that connect business structures.*[1]

Although it's succinct, this definition does not capture the business justification for trying to build an enterprise architecture.

---

[1] Carnegie Mellon University, www.sei.cmu.edu/ architecture/glossary.html.

Wikipedia goes further with its definition of enterprise architecture:

> *The practice of applying a comprehensive and rigorous method for describing a current or future structure for an organization's processes, information systems, personnel and organizational sub-units, so that they align with the organization's core goals and strategic direction.*[2]

The Wikipedia definition gives a better hint of the exhaustive nature of so many enterprise architectures, and even contains a hint as to their value, but it still focuses on the *how* rather than the *why*.

Here is my definition of enterprise architecture, one that focuses on the benefits of an enterprise architecture:

> *An enterprise architecture is a description of the goals of an organization, how these goals are realized by business processes, and how these business processes can be better served through technology.*

In fact, this definition could be simplified even further: enterprise architecture is the art of maximizing the value of IT investments. As I will discuss, the ability to maximize the value of IT investments is largely dependent on our ability to manage the most fundamental impediment to realizing value. But this is getting ahead of the story.

The goal of an enterprise architecture should not be to document every business process, every software system, and every database record that exists throughout the organization. It should be about adding business value.

If adding business value is not the bottom line of an enterprise architecture, the energy put into creating that enterprise architecture has been badly misplaced. If one can achieve this goal without going through a costly, time-consuming process, then I say, so much the better. It is the ends that are important, not the means.

Some of the confusion about enterprise architectures begins with the term *architecture* itself. The word "architecture" implies blueprints. Blueprints are known for their completeness, specifying everything from how the roof connects to the walls, to how the pipes are laid, to where the electrical sockets are located, and so on. Although many enterprise architecture methodologies attempt to capture this level of detail, the effort rarely pays off.

When looking at how to use technology to add business value, we need answers to these questions:

- What are the overall goals of the business?
- How is the business organized into autonomous business processes?

---

[2] Wikipedia, http://en.wikipedia.org/wiki/Enterprise_architecture.

- How are those business processes related to each other?

- Which business processes (or relationships between processes) seem particularly amenable to improvement through technology?

- What is the plan for making those improvements?

There is no such thing as a finished enterprise architecture. Instead, an enterprise architecture should be seen as a living set of documents that guides the use of technology. It is actually much more analogous to a city plan than to a building blueprint.

Using the analogy of a city plan to describe an enterprise architecture was a comparison first made by Armour in 1999[3] and is particularly relevant for today's highly complex organizations.

A city plan addresses different issues than do building blueprints. City plans address issues such as the following:

- What type of buildings will be allowed in which zones (for example, business or residential)?

- How do buildings connect to the city infrastructure (for example, in terms of plumbing and electrical)?

- What impact will buildings have on others of their ilk (for example, on air quality and traffic flow)?

- Are the buildings built to a standard that will not endanger their inhabitants (for example, are they fire and earthquake resistant)?

Imagine a city that included in its city plan a detailed blueprint for every building that would ever be built in the city. Such a plan would be extremely expensive to create, and, if it was ever completed, would be inflexible and stifling. Which, come to think of it, is not unlike some enterprise architectures I have seen.

Complexity in Enterprise Architectures

This field of enterprise architecture was inaugurated more than 20 years ago to address two major problems in the field of information technology that were already becoming apparent. The first problem was managing the increasing complexity of information technology systems. The second problem was the increasing difficulty in delivering real business value with those systems.

---

[3] Arm - A big-picture look at enterprise architectures by Armour, F.J.; Kaisler, S.H.; Liu, S.Y. in IT Professional Volume 1, Issue 1, Jan/Feb 1999 Page(s):35–42.

As you can imagine, these problems are related. The more complex a system, the less likely it is that it will deliver maximum business value. As you better manage complexity, you improve your chances of delivering real business value.

As systems become more complex, they generally require more planning. It is easy to see this in buildings. When Henry David Thoreau built his little cabin on Walden's Pond (shown in Figure 1-1), he embraced simplicity and needed no architects. If you are building New York City (shown in Figure 1-2), simplicity is out of the question and you will need many architects.

FIGURE 1-1 Replica of Thoreau's cabin at Walden Pond.

FIGURE 1-2 New York City.

The relationship between complexity and planning for buildings and cities is similar for information systems. If you are building a simple, single-user, nondistributed system, you might need no architects at all. If you are building an enterprisewide, mission-critical, highly distributed system, you might need a database architect, a solutions architect, an infrastructure architect, a business architect, and an enterprise architect.

This book concerns the responsibilities of the enterprise architect. This is the architect who specializes in the broadest possible view of architecture within the enterprise. This is the architect's architect, the architect who is responsible for coordinating the work of all the other architects. Do you need such an architect? It all depends on what you are building: Thoreau's cabin or New York City.

Building a large complex IT system without an enterprise architect is like trying to build a city without a city planner. Can you build a city without a city planner? Probably. Would you want to live in such a city? Probably not.

Of course, having a city planner does not guarantee a livable city will be built, it merely improves the chances of that happening. Similarly, having an enterprise architect does not guarantee a successful enterprise architecture will be built. There are many examples of failed enterprise architectures in the world today, and all of them had enterprise architects (probably dozens!). But there is one thing that these failed enterprise architects didn't have, and that is a methodology for controlling complexity.

This seems like an odd statement, given that I said that the field of enterprise architecture was started in part, to address the very issue of complexity. However, as I present the major enterprise architectural methodologies in use today, you will notice that none define what complexity looks like, how it should be controlled, or how one can validate that one has successfully eliminated complexity. In fact, most methodologies have become more focused on process rather than deliverables.

And yet, the problem of complexity has never been greater. Over the last decade, the cost and complexity of IT systems have exponentially increased while the chances of deriving real value from those systems have dramatically decreased. The bottom line: more cost, less value. These problems, first recognized 20 years ago, have today reached a crisis point. Large organizations can no longer afford to ignore these problems. The warnings about overcomplexity that 20 years ago seemed quaintly quixotic today seem powerfully prophetic.

Enterprise architectures can be a tremendous asset in finding effective ways to better use technology. You can't afford to ignore the potential of a well-done enterprise architecture. These benefits include decreased costs, improved processes, more agile business solutions, and expanded business opportunities.

But you also can't afford to ignore the risks of getting mired in a bad enterprise architecture. These include astronomical expenses, technological gridlock, and even further diminished

IT credibility. They can also be a huge counterproductive drain on precious organizational resources. All too often, it is this final case that is realized.

What differentiates successful enterprise architectures from unsuccessful ones? In my experience, success in enterprise architecture is almost entirely correlated to complexity. The more complex the enterprise architecture, the less likely the enterprise architecture is to be successful. In other words, the more you need an enterprise architecture, the less likely it is to actually be successful.

As a good example of such failures, we need look no further than the U.S. federal government. It is likely that no organization in the world has dedicated more money, time, and effort to creating and leveraging an effective architecture. How has the U.S. government done?

Apparently, not too well. Hardly a month goes by in which the Government Accountability Office (GAO), an independent watchdog branch of the U.S. government, does not issue a scathing report on the information technology practices of at least one agency. It seems that the more crucial the government agency is, the more likely it is to have major IT failures.

In November 2005, the GAO noted these IT problems with the IRS:

> *The lack of a sound financial management system that can produce timely, accurate, and useful information needed for day-to-day decisions continues to present a serious challenge to IRS management. IRS's present financial management systems...inhibit IRS's ability to address the financial management and operational issues that affect its ability to fulfill its responsibilities as the nation's tax collector.*[4]

The Department of Defense has come under repeated criticism. For example, in June 2005, the GAO issued a report saying

> *DOD's substantial financial and business management weaknesses adversely affect not only its ability to produce auditable financial information, but also to provide accurate, complete, and timely information for management and Congress to use in making informed decisions. Further, the lack of adequate accountability across all of DOD's major business areas results in billions of dollars in annual wasted resources in a time of increasing fiscal constraint and has a negative impact on mission performance.*[5]

---

[4] GAO Report to the Secretary of the Treasury November 2004 FINANCIAL AUDIT IRS's Fiscal Years 2004 and 2003 Financial Statements.

[5] Testimony Before the Subcommittee on Government Management, Finance, and Accountability, Committee on Government Reform, House of Representatives; DOD BUSINESS TRANSFORMATION - Sustained Leadership Needed to Address Long-standing Financial and Business Management Problems (June, 2005).

The highly visible Department of Homeland Security has had many problems. In an August 2004 report, GAO had the following to say:

> [DHS] is missing, either in part or in total, all of the key elements expected to be found in a well-defined architecture, such as descriptions of business processes, information flows among these processes, and security rules associated with these information flows, to name just a few.... Moreover, the key elements that are at least partially present in the initial version were not derived in a manner consistent with best practices for architecture development.... As a result, DHS does not yet have the necessary architectural blueprint to effectively guide and constrain its ongoing business transformation efforts and the hundreds of millions of dollars that it is investing in supporting information technology assets.[6]

The list goes on and on. The FBI has sustained heavy criticism for squandering more than $500 million in a failed effort to create a virtual case filing system. FEMA spent than $100 million on a system that was proven ineffective by Hurricane Katrina. Other federal government groups that have been the subject of GAO criticism include the Census Bureau, Federal Aviation Authority, National Air and Space Administration, Housing and Urban Development, Health and Human Services, Medicare, and Medicaid.

If the federal government is the most comprehensive case study that we have on the value of enterprise architectures, the field is in a pretty sorry state.

Although private industry failures are not as prone to make headlines, the private sector, too, is perfectly capable of bungling enterprise architecture. Private sector failures that seem largely attributed to failures in enterprise architectural methodologies include the following:

- McDonald's failed effort to build an integrated business management system that would tie together its entire restaurant business. Cost: $170 million.[7]

- Ford's failed attempt to build an integrated purchasing system. Cost: $400 million.[8]

- KMart's failed attempt to build a state-of-the-art supply chain management system. Cost: $130 million.[9]

Unfortunately, complexity is not a passing whim. There are three predictions that we can confidently make about the future of enterprise architecture:

- Complexity is only going to get worse.

- If we don't find approaches to managing complexity, we are doomed to fail.

- The existing approaches don't work.

---

[6] GAO Report to the Subcommittee on Technology, Information Policy, Intergovernmental Relations and the Census, Committee on Government Reform, House of Representatives August 2004 HOMELAND SECURITY Efforts Under Way to Develop Enterprise Architecture, but Much Work Remains.

[7] McDonald's: McBusted by Larry Barrett and Sean Gallagher in Baseline, July 2, 2003.

[8] Oops! Ford and Oracle mega-software project crumbles by Patricia Keefe in ADTMag, November 11, 2004.

[9] Code Blue by David F. Carr and Edward Cone in Baseline, November/December 2001.

As Richard Murch succinctly put it in a recent article in *InformIT*:

> *To let IT infrastructures and architectures become increasingly complex with no action is unacceptable and irresponsible. If we simply throw more skilled programmers and others at this problem, chaos will be the order of the day.... Until IT vendors and users alike solve the problem of complexity, the same problems will be repeated and will continue to plague the industry.*[10]

The problem, in a nutshell, is that while organizations have become much more complex in the last 10 years, the methodologies have remained largely stagnant. As The Royal Academy of Engineering and the British Computer Society noted in a 2004 large-scale study of IT complexity:

> *...current software development methods and practices will not scale to manage these increasingly complex, globally distributed systems at reasonable cost or project risk. Hence there is a major software engineering challenge to deal with the inexorable rise in capability of computing and communications technologies.*[11]

My goal in writing this book is to give the practicing enterprise architect some new strategies that are specifically focused on the problem of complexity. But before we discuss these new strategies, let's look at where the field is today, and how it got there.

The Zachman Framework for Enterprise Architectures

The first and most influential enterprise architecture methodology is the Zachman Framework, which was first introduced in 1987 by John Zachman.

The first thing we need to understand about the Zachman Framework is that it isn't a framework, at least by my definition of a framework. According to the American Heritage Dictionary, a framework is defined as

> *A structure for supporting or enclosing something else, especially a skeletal support used as the basis for something being constructed; An external work platform; a scaffold; A fundamental structure, as for a written work; A set of assumptions, concepts, values, and practices that constitutes a way of viewing reality.*[12]

A *taxonomy*, on the other hand, is defined as

> *The classification of organisms in an ordered system that indicates natural relationships; The science, laws, or principles of classification; systematics; Division into ordered groups or categories.*[13]

---

10 Managing Complexity in IT, Part 1: The Problem in InformIT, Oct 1, 2004 By Richard Murch.

11 The Challenges of Complex IT Projects: The report of a working group from The Royal Academy of Engineering and The British Computer Society, April, 2004.

12 "framework." The American Heritage® Dictionary of the English Language, Fourth Edition. Houghton Mifflin Company.

13 "taxonomy." The American Heritage® Dictionary of the English Language, Fourth Edition. Houghton Mifflin Company.

The Zachman "Framework" is actually a taxonomy for organizing architectural artifacts (that is, design documents, specifications, models) that takes into account both whom the artifact targets (for example, business owner, builder) and what particular issue (for example, data, functionality) is being addressed.

As John Zachman retrospectively described his work:

> The [Enterprise Architecture] Framework as it applies to Enterprises is simply a logical structure for classifying and organizing the descriptive representations of an Enterprise that are significant to the management of the Enterprise as well as to the development of the Enterprise's systems.[14]

Many proponents of the Zachman Framework see it as cross disciplinary, with influence extending far beyond IT. One popular book on Zachman, for example, says the following:

> ...in due course, you will discover that the Framework exists in everything you do, not only IT projects. When you thoroughly understand the Framework, you can become more effective in everything you do. This means everything. This statement is not made lightly.[15] [Emphasis in original.]

John Zachman himself told me the following in an interview that I conducted with him:

> ...the Framework schema has been around for thousands of years, and I am sure it will be around for a few more thousands of years. What changes is our understanding of it and how to use it for Enterprise engineering and manufacturing.[15]

Zachman originally explained his IT taxonomy using the building industry as an analogy. In that industry, architectural artifacts are implicitly organized using a two-dimensional grid. One dimension of the grid is the various "players in the game." For a physical building, some of these players are the owner (who is paying for the project), the builder (who is coordinating the overall construction), and a zoning board (who is ensuring that construction follows local building regulations).

A building architect prepares different artifacts for each of these players. Every player demands complete information, but what constitutes completeness differs for the various players. The *owner* is interested in a complete description of the functionality and aesthetics of the building. The *builder* is interested in a complete description of the materials and construction process. The owner doesn't care about the placement of studs in the walls. The builder doesn't care how the bedroom windows line up with the morning sun.

---

[14] The Framework for Enterprise Architecture: Background, Description and Utility by John A. Zachman, published by Zachman Institute for Framework Advancement (ZIFA) Document ID 810-231-0531.

[15] Enterprise Architecture Using the Zachman Framework by Carol O'Rourke, Neal Fishman, and Warren Selkow. Published by Thomson Course Technology 2003. ISBN 0-619-06446-3.

As Zachman said in his original article:

> ...*each of the architectural representations differs from the others in essence, not merely in level of detail.*[16]

The second dimension for architectural artifact organization is the descriptive focus of the artifact—the what, how, where, who, when, and why of the project. This dimension is independent of the first. Both the builder and the owner need to know *what*, but the owner's need to know *what* is different than the builder's need to know *what*. What *what* is what depends on who is asking the question.

In his first paper and Zachman's subsequent elaboration in 1992[17], Zachman proposed that there are six descriptive foci (data, function, network, people, time, and motivation) and six player perspectives (planner, owner, designer, builder, subcontractor, and enterprise). These two dimensions can be arranged in a grid as shown in Figure 1-3.

Take the column describing data, as an example. From the business owner's perspective, "data" means business entities. This can include information about the entities themselves, such as customers and products, or information about relationships between those entities, such as demographic groups and inventories. If you are talking to a business owner about data, this is the language you should use.

From the perspective of the person implementing the database, "data" does not mean business entities, but rows and columns organized into tables and linked together by mathematical joins and projections. If you are talking to a database designer about data, don't talk about customer demographic groups; instead, talk about third-normal relational tables.

It's not that one of these perspectives is better than the other or more detailed than the other or of a higher priority than the other. *Both* of these perspectives on data are critical to a holistic understanding of the system's architecture. As Zachman said:

> *We are having difficulties communicating with one another about information systems architecture, because a set of architectural representations exists, instead of a single architecture. One is not right and another wrong. The architectures are different. They are additive and complementary. There are reasons for electing to expend the resources for developing each architectural representation. And there are risks associated with not developing any one of the architectural representations.*[18]

---

[16] A framework for information systems architecture, by J.A. Zachman in IBM Systems Journal, 26 3, 1987.

[17] Extending and formalizing the framework for information systems architecture, by J.F. Sowa and J.A. Zachman in IBM Systems Journal, 31 3, 1992.

[18] A framework for information systems architecture, by J.A. Zachman in IBM Systems Journal, 26 3, 1987.

As I mentioned earlier, the Zachman Framework consists of six functional foci, each considered from the perspective of a major player. The Zachman framework as it is portrayed today is shown in Figure 1-3.

As you can see in Figure 1-3, there are 36 intersecting cells in a Zachman grid, one for each meeting point between a player's perspective (for example, business owner) and a descriptive focus (for example, data). As we move horizontally (for example, left to right) in the grid, we see different descriptions of the system, all from the same player's perspective. As we move vertically in the grid (for example, top to bottom), we see a single focus but change the player from whose perspective we are viewing that focus.

There are three suggestions of the Zachman grid that can help in the development of an enterprise architecture.

The first suggestion of the Zachman taxonomy is that every architectural artifact should live in one and only one cell. There should be no ambiguity about where a particular artifact lives. If it is not clear in which cell a particular artifact lives, there is most likely a problem with the artifact itself.

As an organization begins accumulating artifacts in the development of an enterprise architecture, it can use the Zachman grid to clarify the focus of each of these artifacts. For example, artifacts relating to a service-oriented architecture live mostly in the third row (designer's perspective). They generally will not be of interest to the business owner.

The second suggestion of the Zachman taxonomy is that an architecture can be considered a *complete* architecture only when every cell in that architecture is complete. A cell is complete when it contains sufficient artifacts to fully define the system for one specific player looking at one specific descriptive focus.

When every cell is populated with appropriate artifacts, there is a sufficient amount of detail to fully describe the system from the perspective of every player (what we might today call a *stakeholder*) looking at the system from every possible angle (descriptive focus). So an organization can use the Zachman grid to ensure that appropriate discussions are occurring between all the important stakeholders of an enterprise architecture.

The third suggestion of the Zachman grid is that cells in columns should be related to each other. Consider, for example, the data column (the first column) of the Zachman grid. From the business owner's perspective, *data* is information about the business. From the database administrator's perspective, data is rows and columns in the database.

Enterprise Architecture - A Framework™

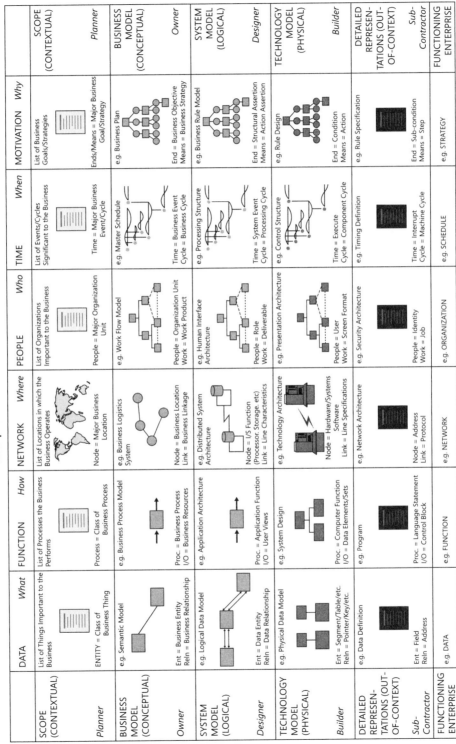

FIGURE 1-3 Zachman grid.

Although the business owner thinks about data quite differently than the database administrator, there should be some relationship between these perspectives. Somebody should be able to follow the business requirements and show that the database design is, in fact, being driven by those requirements. If there are business requirements that are not traceable down to the database design, we must ask if the business needs will be met by this architecture. On the other hand, it there are database design elements that do not trace back to business requirements, we might ask if we have included unnecessary design at the database level.

I see five ways that the Zachman grid can help in the development of an enterprise architecture. It can help

- Ensure that every stakeholder's perspective has been considered for every descriptive focal point.

- Improve the architectural artifacts themselves by sharpening each of their focus points to one particular concern for one particular audience.

- Ensure that all the business requirements can be traced to some technical implementation.

- Convince the business side that the technical team isn't planning on building a bunch of useless functionality.

- Convince the technical team that the business folks are including them in their planning.

But Zachman by itself is not a complete enterprise architectural solution. There are too many critical issues that Zachman does not address. For example, Zachman does not give us a step-by-step process for creating a new architecture. Zachman doesn't give us much help in deciding if the future architecture we are creating is the best architecture possible. For that matter, Zachman doesn't even give us an approach to show a need for a future architecture. And, most importantly, from our perspective, although the Zachman grid might help organize the architectural artifacts, it does nothing to address the complexity of the enterprise that we are trying to understand.

The Open Group Architecture Framework

The Open Group Architecture Framework is best known by its acronym, TOGAF. TOGAF is owned by The Open Group[19], which is a consortium including many vendors and customers. TOGAF's view of an enterprise architecture is shown in Figure 1-4.

---

[19] www.opengroup.org.

Enterprise Architecture

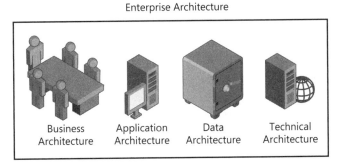

FIGURE 1-4 TOGAF's enterprise architecture.

As shown in this figure, TOGAF divides an enterprise architecture into four categories, as follows:

- **Business architecture**   Describes the processes the business uses to meet its goals

- **Application architecture**   Describes how specific applications are designed and how they interact with each other

- **Data architecture**   Describes how the enterprise data stores are organized and accessed

- **Technical architecture**   Describes the hardware and software infrastructure that supports applications and their interactions

TOGAF describes itself as a "framework," but the most important part of TOGAF is the Architecture Development Method, better known as ADM. ADM is a recipe for creating architecture. A recipe can be categorized as a *process*. Given that ADM is the most visible part of TOGAF, I categorize TOGAF overall as an *architectural process*. I thus reject both the description of TOGAF as either an *architectural framework,* as The Open Group describes TOGAF, or a methodology, as The Open Group describes ADM.

Viewed as an architectural *process*, TOGAF complements Zachman, which, you will recall, I categorized as an architectural *taxonomy*. Zachman tells you how to categorize your artifacts. TOGAF gives you a process for creating them.

TOGAF views the world of enterprise architecture as a continuum of architectures, ranging from highly generic to highly specific. It calls this continuum the *Enterprise Continuum*. It views the process of creating a specific enterprise architecture as moving from the generic to the specific. TOGAF's ADM provides the process for driving this movement.

TOGAF calls most generic architectures *Foundation Architectures*. These are architectural principles that can, theoretically, be used by any IT organization in the universe.

TOGAF calls the next level of specificity *Common Systems Architectures*. These are principles that one would expect to see in many—but perhaps not all—types of enterprises.

TOGAF calls the next level of specificity *Industry Architectures*. These are principles that are specific across many enterprises that are part of the same domain—such as, say, pharmaceutical enterprises.

TOGAF calls the most specific level the *Organizational Architectures*. These are the architectures that are specific to a given enterprise.

Figure 1-5 shows the relationship between the Enterprise Continuum and the Architecture Development Method.

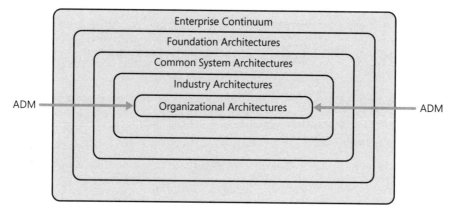

FIGURE 1-5 The TOGAF Enterprise Continuum.

TOGAF defines various knowledge-bases that live in the Foundation Architecture. Two that you might run into are the *Technical Reference Model* (TRM) and the *Standards Information Base* (SIB). The TRM is a suggested description of a generic IT architecture. The SIB is a collection of standards and pseudo-standards that The Open Group recommends that you consider when building an IT architecture.

TOGAF presents both the TRM and the SIB as suggestions; neither is required. In my view, both are biased toward application *portability* at the expense of application *interoperability* and application *autonomy*. I personally consider this an outdated view of technical architectures, but obviously not everybody agrees.

For an enterprise trying to build an enterprise architecture, TOGAF largely boils down to the Architecture Development Method (ADM). Individuals will be exposed to the Enterprise Continuum, the SIB, and the TRM (as well as a few other TOGAF features), which is why I discussed them. But the day-to-day experience of creating an enterprise architecture will be driven by the ADM, a high-level view of which is shown in Figure 1-6.

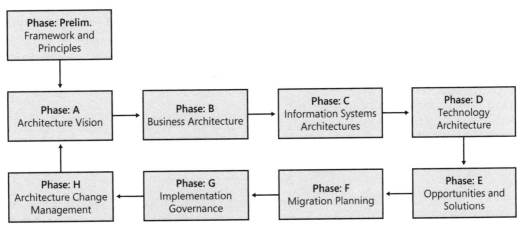

FIGURE 1-6 The TOGAF Architecture Development Method (ADM).

As shown in Figure 1-6, the TOGAF ADM consists of eight phases that are cycled through after an initial "priming of the pump."

The Preliminary Phase typically has three goals:

- To make sure everybody in the organization is comfortable with the process

- To modify the TOGAF process as necessary to fit within the organization's culture

- To set up the governance system that will oversee future architectural work at the organization

In some organizations, achieving buy-in on the need for an enterprise architecture can be very difficult. This is especially true when the effort is driven from the IT organization, and even more so when there is a history of discord between the business and the technical sides of the organization (an all too common situation).

After we have completed the Preliminary Phase, we start Phase A. Phase A begins, at least in theory, with a *Request for Architecture Work* from some group within the organization. This document includes the business reasons for the request, budget and personnel information, and any constraints that need to be considered.

As soon as the Request for Architecture Work (or some equivalent) has been received, we ensure that the project has the necessary support, define the scope of the project, identify constraints, document the business requirements, and establish high-level definitions for both the baseline (starting) architecture and target (desired) architecture.

These baseline and target definitions will include high-level definitions of all four of the enterprise architecture subarchitectures shown back in Figure 1-4—namely, business, technology, data, and application architectures.

The culmination of Phase A will be a Statement of Architecture Work, which must be approved by the various stakeholders before the next phase of the ADM begins. The output of this phase is to create an architectural vision for the first pass through the ADM cycle. An enterprise architect will guide the organization in choosing the project and validating the project against the architectural principles established in the Preliminary Phase. The enterprise architect will also ensure that the appropriate stakeholders have been identified and their issues have been addressed.

The Architectural Vision created in Phase A will be the main input into Phase B. The goal in Phase B is to create a detailed baseline and target business architecture and perform a full analysis of the gaps between them.

Phase B is quite involved—involving business modeling, highly detailed business analysis, and technical requirements documentation. A successful Phase B requires input from many stakeholders. The major outputs will be a detailed description of the baseline and target business objectives, and gap descriptions (that is, descriptions of how to get from the baseline to the target) of the business architecture.

Phase C does for the information systems architecture what Phase B does for the business architecture. In this phase, the enterprise architect works primarily with the technical team. TOGAF defines nine specific steps, each with multiple sub-steps:

1. Develop baseline data architecture description.

2. Review and validate principles, reference models, viewpoints, and tools.

3. Create architecture models, including logical data models, data management process models, and relationship models that map business functions to CRUD (Create, Read, Update, Delete) data operations.

4. Select data-architecture building blocks.

5. Conduct formal checkpoint reviews of the architecture model and building blocks with stakeholders.

6. Review qualitative criteria (for example, performance, reliability, security, integrity).

7. Complete data architecture.

8. Conduct checkpoint/impact analysis.

9. Perform gap analysis.

The most important deliverable from this phase will be the Target Data and Applications Architecture.

Phase D completes the technical architecture—the infrastructure necessary to support the proposed new architecture.

Phase E evaluates the various implementation possibilities, identifies the major implementation projects that might be undertaken, and evaluates the business opportunity associated with each. The TOGAF standard recommends that our first pass at Phase E "focus on projects that will deliver short-term payoffs and so create an impetus for proceeding with longer-term projects."

This is good advice in any architectural methodology. Therefore, we should be looking for projects that can be completed as cheaply as possible while delivering the highest perceived value. A good starting place to look for such projects is the organizational pain-points that initially convinced the organization to adopt an enterprise architectural-based strategy in the first place.

Phase F is closely related to Phase E. In this phase, we work with the organization's governance body to sort the projects identified in Phase E into priority order, which is determined not only by the cost and benefits (identified in Phase E) but also the risk factors.

In Phase G, we take the prioritized list of projects and create architectural specifications for the implementation projects. These specifications will include acceptance criteria and lists of risks and issues.

The final phase is H. In this phase, we modify the architectural change management process with any new artifacts created in this last iteration and with new information that becomes available.

We are now ready to start the cycle again. One of the goals from the first cycle should be information transfer so that outside consulting services are required less and less as more and more iterations of the cycle are completed.

For the most part, the results of the TOGAF process will be determined as much by the individuals in charge of the enterprise architecture as they will by the TOGAF specification itself. TOGAF is meant to be highly adaptable, and details for the various architectural artifacts is sparse. As one book on TOGAF says:

> *TOGAF is not wholly specific with respect to generated documents; in fact, it provides very little in the way of prescriptive document templates—merely guidelines for inputs and outputs.*[20]

The TOGAF specification is also flexible with respect to the phases. As the specification itself says:

> *One of the tasks before applying the ADM is to review its components for applicability, and then tailor them as appropriate to the circumstances of the individual enterprise. This activity might well produce an "enterprise-specific" ADM.*[21]

---

[20] Guide to Enterprise IT Architecture by Col Perks and Tony Beveridge, Springer, published 2003, ISBN 0-387-95132-6.

[21] TOGAF Version 8.1.1.

TOGAF allows phases to be done incompletely, skipped, combined, reordered, or reshaped to fit the needs of the situation. So it should be no surprise if two different TOGAF consultants end up using two very different processes, even when working with the same organization.

TOGAF is even more flexible about the actual generated architecture. In fact, TOGAF is, to a surprising degree, "architecture agnostic." The final architecture might be good, bad, or indifferent. TOGAF merely describes *how* to generate an enterprise architecture, not necessarily how to generate a *good* enterprise architecture. For this, you are dependent on the experience of your staff, TOGAF consultant, or both. People adopting TOGAF hoping to acquire a magic bullet will be sorely disappointed.

And you might also notice a common trend. As with Zachman, TOGAF has no process that specifically focuses on the control of complexity. Like Zachman, it does not model complexity, attempt to understand what causes complexity, or show how the use of the methodology reduces complexity.

Federal Enterprise Architecture

The Federal Enterprise Architecture (FEA) is the latest attempt by the federal government to unite its myriad agencies and functions under a single common and ubiquitous enterprise architecture (EA). FEA is still in its infancy, as most of the major pieces have been available only since 2006. However, it has a long tradition behind it, and, if nothing else, has many failures from which it has hopefully learned some valuable lessons.

FEA is the most complete of all the methodologies discussed in this chapter. It has both a comprehensive taxonomy, like Zachman, and an architectural process, like TOGAF. FEA can be viewed as either a methodology for creating an enterprise architecture or the result of applying that process to a particular enterprise—namely, the U.S. government. I will be looking at FEA from the methodology perspective. My particular interest here is in how can we apply the FEA methodology to private enterprises.

Most writers describe FEA as simply consisting of five reference models, one each for business, service, components, technical, and data. It is true that FEA has these five references models, but there is much more to FEA than just the reference models. A full treatment of FEA needs to include all of the following:

- A perspective on how enterprise architectures should be viewed (the segment model, that I will describe shortly)

- A set of reference models for describing different perspectives of the enterprise architecture (the five models just mentioned)

- A process for creating an enterprise architecture

- A transitional process for migrating from a pre-EA to a post-EA paradigm

- A taxonomy for cataloging assets that fall in the purview of the enterprise architecture

- An approach to measuring the success of using the enterprise architecture to drive business value

You can see that the FEA is about much more than models. It includes everything necessary to build an enterprise architecture for probably the most complex organization on earth: the U.S. government. As the FEA-Program Management Office (FEAPMO) says, FEA, taken *in toto*, provides

> ... *a common language and framework to describe and analyze IT investments, enhance collaboration and ultimately transform the Federal government into a citizen-centered, results-oriented, and market-based organization as set forth in the President's Management Agenda.*[22]

Although it might be a stretch to imagine that anything short of divine intervention could "transform the federal government into a citizen-centered, results-oriented, and market-based organization," there is, at least, hope that some of the FEA methodology could help enterprises deal with the much more mundane problem of aligning business and IT. So, let's take a look at what FEA has to offer.

The FEA perspective on EA is that an enterprise is built of *segments*, an idea first introduced by FEAF[23]. A segment is a major line-of-business functionality, such as human resources. There are two types of segments: *core mission area segments* and *business services segments*.

A *core mission area segment* is one that is central to the mission or purpose of a particular political boundary within the enterprise. For example, in the Health and Human Services (HHS) agency of the federal government, *health* is a core mission area segment.

A *business services segment* is one that is foundational to most, if not all, political organizations. For example, *financial management* is a business services segment that is required by all federal agencies.

Another type of enterprise architecture asset is an *enterprise service*. An enterprise service is a well-defined function that spans political boundaries. An example of an enterprise service is *security management*. Security management is a service that works in a unified manner across the whole swath of the enterprise.

The difference between *enterprise services* and *segments*, especially *business service segments*, is confusing. Both are shared across the entire enterprise. The difference is that business service segments have a scope that encompass only a single political organization. Enterprise services have a scope that encompass the entire enterprise.

---

[22] FEA Consolidated Reference Model Document Version 2.1, December 2006, published by the Federal Enterprise Architecture Program Management Office, Office of Management of Budget.

[23] A Practical Guide to Federal Enterprise Architecture by the CIO Council, Version 1.0, February 2001.

In the federal government, for example, both HHS and the Environmental Protection Agency (EPA) use the business service segment *human resources*. However, the people who are managed by human resources are in a different group for HHS than they are for the EPA.

Both HHS and the EPA also use the enterprise service *security management*. But the security credentials that are managed by the security management service are not specific to either of those agencies. Security credentials are managed effectively only when they are managed at the scope of the enterprise.

Resist the temptation to equate either *segments* or *services* with services as in *service-oriented architectures*. There are two reasons such a comparison would be flawed. First, enterprise services, business-service segments, and core mission-area segments are all much broader in focus than services found in service-oriented architectures. Second, segments are an organizational unit for an *enterprise architecture*, whereas services are an organizational unit for *technical implementations*. As organizational units for an enterprise architecture, their depth includes not just the technical, but also the business and the data architectures.

One final note about segments: although segments function at the political (that is, agency) level, they are defined at the enterprise (that is, government) level. Enterprise services, of course, both function and are defined at the enterprise level.

The fact that segments are defined globally facilitates their reuse across political boundaries. One can map out the usage of segments across the political boundaries of the enterprise and then use that map to seek opportunities for architectural reuse. Figure 1-7, for example, shows a segment map of the federal government from the FEA Practice Guide[24]. As you can see, there are many segments (the vertical columns) that are used in multiple agencies and any or all of these are good candidates for sharing.

The five FEA reference models are all about establishing common languages. The goal here is to facilitate communication, cooperation, and collaboration across political boundaries. According to the FEAPMO:

> The FEA consists of a set of interrelated "reference models" designed to facilitate cross-agency analysis and the identification of duplicative investments, gaps and opportunities for collaboration within and across agencies. Collectively, the reference models comprise a framework for describing important elements of the FEA in a common and consistent way.[25]

---

[24] FEA Practice Guidance, December 2006, published by the Federal Enterprise Architecture Program Management Office, Office of Management of Budget.

[25] FEA Consolidated Reference Model Document Version 2.1, December 2006, published by the Federal Enterprise Architecture Program Management Office, Office of Management of Budget.

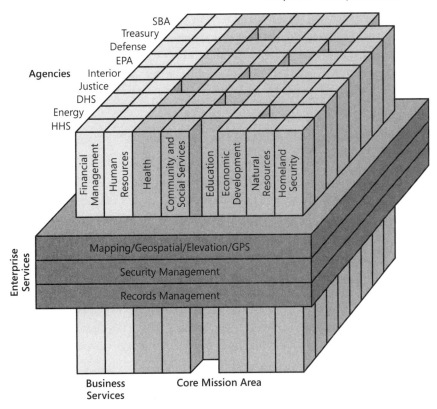

FIGURE 1-7 Segment map of the federal government.

Why do we need a common language? Consider this exchange:

James: Do you have a torch I can borrow?

Roger: No, I'm afraid not.

James: Do you know where I can get one?

Roger: The hardware store in town should have one.

So James goes out to the hardware store and buys himself a torch. He returns.

Roger: Did you get your torch?

James: Yes, here it is.

Roger: That's not a torch! That's a flashlight. Why didn't you say so? I have one you could have borrowed.

James: Well why didn't you say so?

The problem, of course, is that James comes from England where what I call a *flashlight*, they call a *torch*. And when I hear *torch*, I think of a *blowtorch*. Although we both speak English, we don't necessarily speak the same English. The result is that James goes out and unnecessarily spends money on something that I could have lent him.

This is exactly the problem that the FEA Reference Models are trying to solve on a much larger scale. Suppose the Internal Revenue Service (IRS) decides it needs a *demographics* system to track taxpayer data. They ask around to see if anybody has one they can modify for their purposes. Nobody does.

Little do they know that right next door the Government Printing Office (GPO) has a perfectly good demographics system that is almost exactly what the IRS needs. They just happen to call it a *customer analytics* system.

So, the IRS goes out and builds its system from scratch rather than simply modifying the one already built (and paid for) by the GPO. And, in doing so, the IRS will waste considerably more money than James spent on his unnecessary flashlight.

This, in a nutshell, is the goal of the five FEA reference models: to give standard terms and definitions for the domains of enterprise architecture and thereby facilitate collaboration and sharing across the federal government. The five reference models are as follows:

- The *Business Reference Model (BRM)* gives a business view of the various functions of the federal government. For example, the BRM defines a standard business capability called *water resource management* that is a sub-function of *natural resources* that is considered a *line-of-business* of the broader business area *services for citizens.*[26]

- The *Components Reference Model (CRM)* gives a more IT-oriented view of systems that can support business functionality. For example, the CRM defines a *customer analytics* system, which I mentioned earlier in the hypothetical interchange between the Internal Revenue Service and the Government Printing Office.[27]

- The *Technical Reference Model (TRM)* defines the various technologies and standards that can be used in building IT systems. For example, the TRM defines HTTP as a *protocol* that is a subset of a *service transport* that is a subset of *service access and delivery.*[28]

- The *Data Reference Model (DRM)* defines standard ways of describing data. For example, the DRM defines an *entity* as something that *contains attributes* and *participates in relationships.*[29]

---

[26] ibid.

[27] ibid.

[28] ibid.

[29] The Data Reference Model, Version 2.0, November 2005, published by the Federal Enterprise Architecture Program Management Office, Office of Management of Budget.

- The *Performance Reference Model (PRM)* defines standard ways of describing the value delivered by enterprise architectures. For example, the PRM describes *quality* as a technology measurement area that is defined as "the extent to which technology satisfies functionality or capability requirements."[30]

The FEA process is primarily focused on creating a segment architecture for a subset of the overall enterprise (in FEA's case, the enterprise is the federal government and the subset is a governmental agency) and is described in the FEA Practice Guidance[31]. I discussed the FEA vision on enterprise segments earlier. The overall segment-architecture development process is (at a very high level) as follows:

- **Step 1: Architectural Analysis**   Define a simple and concise vision for the segment, and relate it back to the organizational plan.

- **Step 2: Architectural Definition**   Define the desired architectural state of the segment, document the performance goals, consider design alternatives, and develop an enterprise architecture for the segment, including business, data, services, and technology architectures.

- **Step 3: Investment and Funding Strategy**   Consider how the project will be funded.

- **Step 4: Program Management Plan and Execution of Projects**   Create a plan for managing and executing the project, including milestones and performance measures that will asses project success.

The FEA framework for measuring organizational success in using enterprise architecture is defined in the Federal Enterprise Architecture Program EA Assessment Framework 2.1[32]. Federal agencies are rated as to their overall maturity levels in three main categories:

- **Architectural completion**   Maturity level of the architecture itself

- **Architectural use**   How effectively the agency uses its architecture to drive decision-making

- **Architectural results**   The benefits being realized by the use of the architecture

The Office of Management and Budget (OMB) assigns each agency a success rating, based on its scores in each category and a cumulative score, as follows:

- **Green**   The agency rates quite well in the *completion* area. (It has a quite mature enterprise architecture.) It also rates well in both the *use* area (that is, it is effectively using that enterprise architecture to drive ongoing strategy) and the *results* area (that is, the usage of that architecture is driving business value).

---

[30] FEA Consolidated Reference Model Document Version 2.1, December 2006, published by the Federal Enterprise Architecture Program Management Office, Office of Management of Budget.

[31] FEA Practice Guidance, December 2006, published by the Federal Enterprise Architecture Program Management Office, Office of Management of Budget.

[32] Federal Enterprise Architecture Program EA Assessment Framework 2.1, Dec 2006.

- **Yellow** The agency rates quite well in the *completion* area. It also rates well in either the *use* area or the *results* area.

- **Red** The agency does not have a completed architecture, is not effectively using that architecture, or both.

The framework is interesting beyond the confines of the public sector. The category ratings can be fruitfully adapted by many enterprises to assess the maturity level of their own architectural efforts. Figure 1-8, for example, shows my own interpretation of the OMB maturity rankings for *architectural completion* as I adapt them for the private sector. Similar adaptations can be created for *architectural usage* and *architectural results*.

This completes the discussion of FEA. As you can see, FEA includes quite a bit of methodology.

The one thing that FEA does not include is a methodology that specifically addresses how one manages complexity. In this one regard, FEA is just like Zachman and TOGAF. And it is in the failure to control complexity that one can find the root cause of so many enterprise architecture failures of the U.S. government.

Category: Architectural Completion

Description: This category measures the architectural maturity of an enterprise's architecture in terms of performance, business, data, service, and technology. This includes an assessment of the architectural artifacts and both the baseline (existing) and target (goal) architectures.

Level	Name	Description
1	Initial	The enterprise is using informal and ad-hoc EA processes. Some architectural artifacts for a given architectural level may exist, but the levels are not linked or the linkage is incomplete.
2	Baseline	The enterprise has developed a baseline (as-is) architecture. The architecture has enterprisewide scope, and the linkages between levels are well established and clearly articulated.
3	Target	The enterprise has developed both a baseline architecture (as described above) and a target (goal) architecture. The target architecture is aligned to enterprisewide goals and organizational responsibilities. The target architecture addresses the priorities and performance objectives identified in the enterprise business plan.
4	Integrated	The enterprise has developed at least vertically partitioned architecture that has been approved by the business owner in writing. The relevant organization(s) within the enterprise are actively migrating toward the relevant architecture.
5	Optimized	The enterprise has developed multiple vertically partitioned architectures that support core mission business functions, all approved by the appropriate business owners.

FIGURE 1-8 OMB Ranking of Architectural Completion, adapted for the private sector by Roger Sessions.

Summary

I have given you an overview of some of the problems that drive organizations to consider enterprise architectures and described the commonly used enterprise architectural methodologies—the three most popular being Zachman, TOGAF, and FEA.

The original goal of enterprise architecture was to address the growing rift between technological capability and business need in an environment in which both were becoming increasingly complex. And while all of the existing enterprise architecture methodologies claim to help address complexity, none of the existing methodologies do so in any meaningful way.

It's easy to understand why none of these methodologies attempt to address complexity. The problem of complexity is, well, complex. But that is, indeed, the problem we need to understand if we are to leverage enterprise architectures in any meaningful way. So the problem of complexity is where we go next.

Chapter 2
A First Look at Complexity

We don't need to look very far to find complexity. It is all around us. It is in the stores at which we shop, the organizations to which we belong, and the enterprises at which we work.

In general, it is easy to understand how things get more complex. If you have a bucket of stuff and add more stuff to the bucket, the bucket becomes more complex. As the bucket becomes more complex, it becomes more difficult to manage the bucket.

Any parent knows that the more children whose needs you are trying to juggle, the more harried your life becomes. A large department store with thousands of items for sale is more difficult to manage than a small coffee shop with dozens of items for sale. A group with 30 people has more difficulty reaching a decision than does a group of three people. A large IT system with many functions is more difficult to maintain than a small system with fewer functions.

 The rules that govern complexity for all of these systems are essentially the same. The approaches that help us reduce complexity in a department store can be used to reduce complexity in IT systems, once we understand what those rules are. So in this chapter, I will look at some of the everyday strategies that we use to manage complexity in our daily lives.

Partitioning

Let's start with the most important of the complexity control strategies: partitioning. Partitioning refers to the process of taking a group of items and dividing them into smaller, subgroups of items. If this subdividing process follows certain rules, the result is a substantial reduction in complexity. Reduced complexity frequently results in improved efficiency. How this efficiency manifests itself depends on the system in question. Let's consider some examples of partitioning.

Executive Lunch

You are in a meeting with 20 high-ranking executives. The meeting is scheduled to last all day. Lunch will be served. The first order of business is to decide on the lunch menu. The only rule is that all attendees must agree on the menu. How can we do this?

We could start the meeting by discussing the lunch menu. We could allow attendees to make suggestions. We could discuss those suggestions. After we achieve consensus, we could finalize the menu and go on to the rest of our business.

This would be a highly inefficient way to plan lunch. Likely, lunch time would come and go with no lunch plan.

Another approach is to use partitioning. In this approach, we divide the 20 executives into five groups of four, with each group assigned one part of the lunch menu. Group 1 gets to decide on appetizers. Group 2 determines salads. Group 3 decides on side dishes. Group 4 decides on the main course. Group 5 makes the decision about dessert.

This approach is much more efficient than the first one mentioned. Although few people would think the outcome (lunch) was perfect, all would feel it was good enough. And all would be grateful that the time (and aggravation) needed to reach agreement was minimized.

The reason the partitioned approach works so much better than the nonpartitioned approach is because it is so much simpler. It is simpler because each executive gets input on only one lunch item and each lunch item is beholden to a much smaller group of executives. If the desired outcome of this system is to design a lunch menu, the partitioned approach is clearly superior to the nonpartitioned approach.

Choir Rehearsal

Consider singing in a choir. If you have ever sung in a choir, you know that most choral music is four parts: soprano, alto, tenor, and bass. There are two approaches that I have seen for choir direction.

The first approach is to rehearse the choir en masse, letting each choir member pick out his or her own part as best he or she can. When one group needs to hear its own part, the other groups sit around waiting or, if they are sopranos, talking among themselves.

The second approach is to split the four groups. In this approach, each group learns its own part by itself, working with its own section leader. There are no distractions, and there is no downtime while waiting for other groups. Once each group knows its part, the choir comes together and the choir director applies the final touches.

The second approach is simpler. Each group learns its part without distractions and without downtime. Even though each group is giving up time with the more experienced choir director to work with a less experienced section leader, the net effect is still greater, not less, efficiency.

When the goal of this system is to perform music, the partitioned approach is superior. Nobody in the choir is perfectly happy. Each group might have preferred to have the full attention of the choir director. But the net result is faster learning. Partitioning provides a solution that makes the most efficient use of the time available.

Emergency Responses

Those unlucky enough to be involved in a major car accident know that the emergency response protocol has some well-defined stages, which can be summarized something like this:

- The patient is removed from the car.
- The car is towed away.
- The patient is transported to the hospital.
- The patient is admitted to the hospital.
- The patient is treated.
- The patient is given care instructions.
- The patient is released.

Dozens of people are involved in the aftermath of a major car accident, including police, firefighters, emergency medical technicians, nurses, x-ray technicians, surgeons, anesthesiologists, and tow-truck operators, to name just a few. Imagine the pandemonium that would result if all these people converged on the scene of the wreck and followed the patient through each step of the protocol. We would have the x-ray technician arguing with the nurse about how best to direct traffic. We would have the tow-truck operator debating the surgeon on how best to remove the patient from the car.

You do not want a surgeon removing you from the car. Even though a surgeon has at least 10 years of post high-school education and experience, a surgeon is not trained in removing an injured person from a wrecked car.

You would prefer to have an emergency response technician remove you from the car. Even though that person might have no formal education beyond high school, the emergency response person has the knowledge, experience, and tools to remove a crash victim from a car, stabilize that person, and prepare him or her for transport.

You also don't want the surgeon transporting you to the hospital. You want somebody transporting you who is trained in emergency driving, who knows the road conditions, traffic conditions, which hospitals are nearby, and which hospitals are best for which types of injuries.

In fact, in the entire treatment protocol, there is really only one phase for which the caregiver of choice is a highly trained surgeon. That is the relatively limited time that you are actually being treated in the operating room.

The reasons that emergency response systems work well is not because of the number of people involved in a typical rescue. The system works well because the system is carefully partitioned into phases of the rescue, and each phase of the rescue is assigned to somebody who can do that particular job well.

Clothing Store

We could create a clothing store in which every item you could want is located within 100 feet of the entrance. All that is required is to take every item the stores sells and put it in a large, random pile at the front of the store.

But having to go through a random pile of clothes doesn't appeal to most people. We think it is better to have all the men's clothes together in one section, the women's clothes in another section, and so on. Even within the men's section, we like to see clothing organized by type, such as sports clothes, business suits, and so on. And even within the type, we like to see all of the blue jeans together, sorted by manufacturer and then by size.

Retail stores make extensive use of partitions. They know that the simplification that results from partitioning greatly outweighs the benefits of having every item within 100 feet of the store entrance. The partitioned system is simpler and, therefore, much more efficient.

Chess Games

Sometimes partitions show up in the most unexpected places. I was recently playing an online game of chess with Al Summers, a composer and music teacher in Wiltshire, England. I had managed to get myself into quite a quagmire, as shown in Figure 2-1. I was playing white, Al was playing black, and it was my turn.

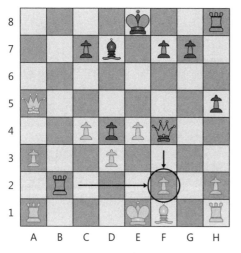

FIGURE 2-1 Roger's quagmire.

Now before I get too far in this discussion, let me issue a disclaimer: if you are not interested in chess, feel free to skip this example. It isn't critical, but it is fun. At least, for some of us!

Notice the bottom four rows of the board (rows 1 through 4) in Figure 2-1. See how Al's black rook at B2 and queen at F4 were ganging up on my white pawn at F1? Although my queen was nearby at A5, her movement was constricted and my two rooks at A1 and H1 were serving mainly as passive spectators. If Al's queen took my F2 pawn, I would have no choice but to move my king to D1. Al would then move his queen to D2 for checkmate.

But what could I do? I had no way to capture Al's queen or rook and I had no protection for my pawn at F2. Things were looking pretty bleak.

Just as I was getting ready to resign, I noticed my white bishop at F1. Although my bishop couldn't take either the B2 rook or the F4 queen or defend the F2 pawn, he could interpose himself between the rook and the queen. Moving my bishop from F1 to E2 gave the position shown in Figure 2-2.

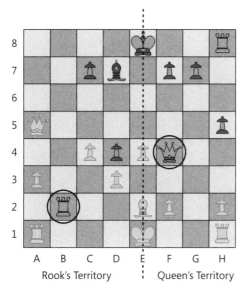

FIGURE 2-2 Position after bishop move.

Although moving the bishop neither threatened nor protected anybody, it did something perhaps even better. It *partitioned* the board so that the black rook's territory of influence was separated from the black queen's territory of influence. The queen could still take the F2 pawn, but the rook would no longer reinforce the queen. In fact, had Al made this move (he didn't, unfortunately) my king would have been able to take his queen. The ability of the bishop to *partition* the board saved the game for me!

Children at Starbucks

As I am writing this in my local Starbucks, I am watching a number of children running back and forth between the pastry case, the bathroom, the tables, and the comfortable easy chairs. Several harried mothers are trying desperately to keep track of their children. Why is this scene so chaotic? Starbucks is very well partitioned, with each table a subset of its own.

Unfortunately, for the mothers who are trying to talk among themselves, children do not respect the partitions. They are free and exuberant. They are chaos incarnate. Perhaps sometimes we take our partitions too seriously!

Rubik's Cube

I was recently comparing notes on complexity with Kevin Drinkwater, the Chief Information Officer (CIO) of Mainfreight whom I mentioned in the preface. Kevin had another interesting analogy for complexity. He suggested that you consider a Rubik's Cube. A Rubik's Cube is a Cube in which each of the six sides is composed of 3-by-3 cells. Your goal is to rotate bands of the Cube until each side of the Cube contains cells of only one particular color. The standard Rubik's Cube is shown in Figure 2-3.

FIGURE 2-3 A 3-by-3 Rubik's Cube.

> **Note** Rubik's Cube (R) used by permission of Seven Towns, Ltd. For more information, visit *www.rubiks.com*.

If you have ever tried to solve a Rubik's Cube, you know how difficult it is. For those of us who are Rubik's Cube challenged, there is another form of a Rubik's Cube with 2-by-2 cells. This version is called a Pocket Cube and is shown in Figure 2-4.

FIGURE 2-4 A 2-by-2 Rubik's Cube.

As you can see from Figures 2-3 and 2-4, the 3-by-3 Cube has 27 interior Cubes and the 2-by-2 Cube has 8 interior Cubes. In general, an *N*-by-*N* Rubik's Cube has N3 interior Cubes.

If you are a true Rubik's Cube masochist, there is a 4-by-4 Rubik's Cube. (Yes, there really is such a thing!) The 4-by-4 Cube contains 4 × 4 × 4, or 64, interior Cubes. The complexity of the 4-by-4 Cube makes the 3-by-3 Cube look like a walk in the park.

The 4-by-4 Rubik's Cube has an interesting relationship to the 2-by-2 Cube: if we dissect the 4-by-4 Cube and reform the 64 interior Cubes into 2-by-2 Cubes, we need exactly eight of the 2-by-2 Cubes to hold all the original interior Cubes.

Which do you think is more complex, the eight 2-by-2 Cubes or the one 4-by-4 Cube? Keep in mind that both systems have the same number of interior Cubes, 64. And if you think the 4-by-4 Cube is more complex, take a guess as to how much more complex it is before you continue.

According to Wikipedia, a 4-by-4 Cube has 7.4×10^{45} possible permutations. That is approximately 7,400,000,000,000,000,000,000,000,000,000,000,000,000,000,000 possible ways the cells might find themselves arranged. If you will be trying these randomly (as I would), you have a lot of trials ahead of you.

A 2-by-2 Cube, on the other hand, has "only" 3.7×10^{6} permutations. But we don't have just one of these to solve, we have eight. So the number of permutations is $8 \times 3.7 \times 10^{6}$, or 29.6×10^{6}, or (just to keep the numbers lined up) 2.96×10^{7}. This is approximately 29,600,000 different possibilities.

So while eight 2-by-2 Cubes is very complex (as measured by the 2.96×10^{7} permutations), it is trivial compared to a single 4-by-4 Cube (as measured by the 7.4×10^{45} permutations). How much simpler are the eight 2-by-2 Cubes relative to the one 4-by-4 Cube?

The formula for determining the relative complexity is as follows:

$(2.96 \times 10^{7}/7.4 \times 10^{45}) \times 100$

This number is 4.0×10^{35}. So the 4-by-4 Cube is 4.0×10^{35} times more complex than the eight 2-by-2 Cubes.

It's hard to grasp numbers of this magnitude, so let's look at it on a different scale. If the combined complexity of the eight 2-by-2 Cubes is defined to be one millimeter (about .04 inch), the relative complexity of the one 4-by-4 Cube is further away than the most distant star that can be seen using the most powerful telescopes available today.

In other words, by partitioning the 64 interior Cubes of a 4-by-4 Rubik's Cube into eight 2-by-2 Rubik's Cubes, we don't just reduce the overall complexity of the system, we slash it by astronomical proportions.

Here's another interesting side note about these Cubes. Whereas the 4-by-4 Rubik's Cube is so complex that the task of solving it should be undertaken only by the most dedicated fanatics, the 2-by-2 Rubik's Cube is recommended for "eight year olds through adults." So while I have still yet to successfully solve my "simple" 2-by-2 Rubik's Cube, this statement gives me great hope. My 4-by-4 Cube, on the other hand, just sits on my desk as a monument to the hopelessness of unchecked complexity.

Sorry, I promised to hold off on the math until the next chapter, but I couldn't resist giving you this peek at the awesome power of partitioning.

As you can see, partitioning is a basic approach that we use every day in managing the complexity of our lives. In fact, given the pervasive nature of partitioning, it is somewhat remarkable that we have not used it more effectively in enterprise architectures.

Five Laws of Partitions

If we consider the examples of partitioned systems I have discussed (executive lunch, choir, and so on), a set of common laws emerges. I'll give each of these a formal name because I will refer to them throughout the remainder of this book. I'll start by listing the five laws, and then we'll look at each in more detail:

- **First Law of Partitions**   Partitions must be true partitions.
- **Second Law of Partitions**   Partition definitions must be appropriate to the problem at hand.
- **Third Law of Partitions**   The number of subsets in a partition must be appropriate.
- **Fourth Law of Partitions**   The size of the subsets in a partition must be roughly equal.
- **Fifth Law of Partitions**   The interactions between subsets in the partitions must be minimal and well defined.

First Law: Partitions Must Be True Partitions

The first law of partitions states that all partitions must be valid partitions as defined by the mathematical rules laid down by set theory. I will discuss these mathematical rules in detail in the next chapter. For now, think of a partition as a way of dividing a collection of things into subsets so that any one of those things lives in one subset only. We see this in each of the examples given earlier.

The executive lunch planning worked well because every executive was assigned one and only one group (subset), and that group was given specific responsibility for one and only one part of the meal. Had the executives been able to freely move from one group to another, the lunch planning process would not have been improved by the partitioning.

The choir rehearsal worked well because every member of the choir is assigned one and only one voice group (tenor, soprano, and so on) and each voice group (subset) works independently of the others. If the sopranos had been free to barge in on the tenor practice session, the tenors would have been no better off than they were in the full session.

The emergency response system works well because every person in the response team knows exactly when his or her responsibilities start and, just as importantly, when they end.

The responsibilities are partitioned into subsets. A surgeon provides value in the operating room but just gets in the way at the accident scene.

The clothing store organization works well because every item of clothing lives in one and only one store location (subset). A system in which some men's dress shirts are located in sporting goods and others are located in infant clothing has little value, at least to those looking for men's dress shirts.

My chess game worked because the bishop partitioned the chess board so that the rook and the queen each lived in its own area (subset), and the influence of each was limited to that area. If the bishop had not been where he was, the game would have gone quite differently.

The partitioning of the 4-by-4 Rubik's Cube worked well because each of the 64 interior Cubes was assigned one and only one of the eight 2-by-2 Rubik's Cubes. If the interior Cubes had the ability to somehow float back and forth between one 2-by-2 Cube and another, we would be no better off with our smaller Cubes.

Second Law: Partition Definitions Must Be Appropriate

The second law of partitions states that all partitions must be appropriate to the problem at hand. Partitions are not helpful if they don't make sense.

Suppose we defined our choir practice groups to be assigned, not by voice type, but by age. Those between 0 and 20 years of age practice with Group One, Those between 21 and 30 years practice with Group Two, and so on. Although this is still a *valid* partition in the sense that every member of the choir lives in one and only one group (and thus respects the First Law of Partitions), it is not an *appropriate* partition. It buys us nothing in terms of expediting our choir rehearsal.

Similarly, suppose we assign emergency response personnel, not by skill, but by last name. The first group, determined by alphabet, removes the patient from the automobile. The second alphabetically arranged group transports the patient to the hospital, and so on. Although this, too, is valid partitioning (again, based on the First Law), it, too, is an *inappropriate* partition. It does not help in our ultimate goal of rescuing victims of car crashes.

If the clothing store is organized, say, by fabric color, we would still have a highly organized (that is, partitioned) store, but it would be a partition that would be of little value in helping customers find what they want.

As you can see, partitions by themselves do not minimize complexity. They only do so when they are appropriate to the problem at hand. This leads to an interesting question. If there is more than one way to partition a number of items, how do you know which of these is the approach that is appropriate to the problem at hand? For the answer to this question, you need to wait until the next chapter.

Third Law: Partition Subset Numbers Must Be Appropriate

In most situations, there seems to be an optimum number of partition subsets. Adding more subsets (and thereby reducing the number of items in each subset) seems to reduce complexity slightly or not at all. Reducing the number of subsets (and thereby increasing the number of elements in each subset) seems to add complexity.

In the executive lunch scenario, I would expect a huge reduction in complexity (measured in time required to order lunch) in going from one subset (all executives order everything) to five subsets (four executives per group). I doubt that there would be much of a further reduction if we went to three executives per group, and I would expect to see increased complexity as we added more subsets beyond that. Of course, this is mostly speculative. It's hard to get executives to cooperate in this experiment!

In the choir scenario, the ideal number of subsets in the partition is obviously fixed at four, corresponding to the four voice parts. Splitting up the tenors is unlikely to significantly improve the situation. Of course, splitting up the sopranos is *always* tempting.

So although I can't yet give rules for determining the optimal number of partitions for all systems, I suspect that most systems have natural fracture lines that you can discern by allowing yourself to study the system in question. In the next chapter, we will see how in the specific case of enterprise architectures we can use mathematical equivalence relations to determine the optimal number of subsets in the partition.

Fourth Law: Partition Subset Sizes Must Be Roughly Equal

For most systems, the elements in each partition subset should be roughly equivalent in both cardinality (the number of elements per subset) and stature (the importance of each element collection in each subset).

If we, for example, ended up with eight executives in the dessert group, we might have lunch at noon, but we could be eating cheesecake the following week.

If our choir had 100 sopranos and 5 tenors, the poor tenors would be overwhelmed.

In the emergency response system, if we had 20 surgeons all in charge of the same operating room, we would have confusion over whose orders should be given priority.

If our clothing store is 99 percent women's clothes and 1 percent men's clothes, the men are going to shop elsewhere.

If my chess game had been partitioned so that both the rook and the queen were on the same side of the partition, my partitioning of the board would have achieved nothing.

So although it is not necessary for all partition subsets to have an identical number of elements (the men won't notice if the store is 49 percent men's clothing and 51 percent women's clothing), it does seem to be necessary, as far as managing complexity, that the sizes of the subsets and their importance in the overall partition be roughly equivalent.

Fifth Law: Subset Interactions Must Be Minimal and Well Defined

A reduction in complexity is dependent on minimizing both the number and the nature of interactions between the subsets of the partition.

With the executive lunch scenario, the system works best when each group deliberates independently. If the dessert group listens in on the entrée group's deliberations and starts basing its choices on the current state of the entrée discussion, the system as a whole breaks down. The system works best when each planning group works independently.

With the choir, if the tenors can clearly hear the sopranos in the next room, their ability to focus is compromised. The system works best when the groups practice in complete isolation from each other and come together only at the end, when each group knows its part.

With the emergency response system, if the surgeon gives directions on removing the victim from the car or the tow-truck operator administers anesthesia in the operating room, the system (and the patient) will quickly deteriorate. The emergency response system works best only when each person works within his or her proscribed subset.

And so, too, with the other examples. In the clothing store, if the store personnel don't take active measures to maintain the partitions (that is, return clothing to the appropriate locations), the system will quickly break down. In my chess game with Al, if the rook could have found a way to pass through the bishop, my game would have quickly ended.

Simplification

Partitioning, as you have seen, is an incredibly effective approach to reducing complexity. But there is usually more we can do to reduce complexity, and that is apply simplification algorithms.

There are two general simplification algorithms we use in our everyday lives, although we don't think of them in formal terms. One is the removal of partition subsets along with their associated items. The other is the removal of items from one or more partition subsets, leaving the subsets themselves in place. In both cases, we must remove as much as possible, but not too much. We are always looking for a balance.

Let's return to the executive lunch scenario. Removing partition subsets is equivalent to partitioning the executives into groups, as before, but now assigning lunch responsibility to only one of the subsets. Removing items from the partition subsets is equivalent to removing executives from each group, and thus having fewer executives offering opinions on each of the lunch choices.

In the case of the executive lunch, we will probably do both. The ideal lunch planning approach is to remove all but one partition and all but one executive. Typically, this is exactly how executive lunches are planned. One executive (or that executive's assistant) makes all the lunch decisions.

In the case of the emergency response system, we try to simplify the system by encouraging the use of seat belts, air bags, and driver training. The goal of all of these measures is to eliminate the hospital subset altogether.

In the case of the clothing store, multiple approaches are used. Some stores use subset elimination, say, selling only children's clothing. Others maintain large numbers of partitions but limit the items in each partition, say, by selling only inexpensive clothing, only clothing aimed at certain demographic groups, or only clothing for certain sizes.

In the case of my chess game, I tried to reduce the complexity of the system by eliminating either Al's rook or queen. Unfortunately, Al was uncooperative.

Iteration

After we have completed the partitioning and simplification phases, we are still left with a number of minimally complex collections that must now be implemented. We have two choices as to how we can do this. We can implement *iteratively* or *noniteratively*.

In an iterative solution, we choose one of the partition subsets from among those awaiting implementation. We then fully implement it. We then go to the next subset from among those still awaiting implementation. We then fully implement it. We continue this until all subsets are implemented.

In a noniterative solution, we choose a bit from each of the subsets and implement it. We then choose another bit from each of the subsets and implement it. We continue this until all the bits of all the subsets are implemented.

The iterative approach results in the delivery of a larger number of smaller pieces. The noniterative approach results in the delivery of a smaller number (often one) of larger pieces.

In the iterative solution, the subsets of the partition roll out one at a time. In the noniterative solution, the subsets are all rolled out at the same time, an approach that I call *big-bang delivery*.

A few years ago, John Cavnar-Johnson introduced me to a fascinating study on iterative versus noniterative solutions by a guy named John Boyd, pictured in Figure 2-5. This study has shaped much of my thinking on the topic of iteration in enterprise architectures.

FIGURE 2-5 John Boyd

John Boyd was not an enterprise architect. He was an Air Force Colonel. And he wasn't interested in IT architectures. He was interested in how to win dogfights.

A dogfight is a one-on-one battle between two fighter pilots, each trying to shoot the other down before he, himself, is shot down. You can see why an Air Force Colonel might be interested in winning them.

Boyd was interested not just in any dogfight, but specifically in dogfights between MiG-15s and F-86s. As an ex-pilot and accomplished aircraft designer, Boyd knew both planes very well. He knew the MiG-15 (shown in Figure 2-6) was a better aircraft than the F-86 (shown in Figure 2-7). The MiG-15 could climb faster than the F-86. The MiG-15 could turn faster than the F-86. The MiG-15 had better distance visibility.

FIGURE 2-6 A MiG-15 cockpit.

FIGURE 2-7 An F-86 cockpit.

There was just one problem with all of this. Even though the MiG-15 was considered a superior aircraft by Boyd and most other aircraft designers, the F-86 was preferred by pilots. The reason it was preferred was simple: in one-on-one dogfights with MiG-15s, the F-86 won nine times out of ten.

This problem fascinated Boyd. Why would an inferior aircraft consistently win over a superior aircraft?

To understand this anomaly, Boyd needed to understand how pilots actually operate in dogfights. Boyd had an advantage here. He was not only a pilot, but one of the best dogfighters in history. He therefore had some firsthand knowledge of the subject.

Let's consider a pilot involved in a dogfight, we'll call him Pete. Boyd proposed that Pete's dogfight consists of four distinct stages. In the first stage, Pete observes the state of the world around him, including the enemy plane. In the second stage, Pete orients himself with respect to that state. In the third stage, Pete plans on an appropriate action. In the fourth stage, Pete acts.

So Pete first observes, then orients, then plans, then acts. Boyd called this sequence OOPA (observe, orient, plan, act).

> **Note** Readers familiar with Boyd's work might recognize that Boyd called his loop OODA for Observe, Orient, Deploy, Act. However, I have change the *deploy* to *plan* for two reasons. First, technology readers will be confused by the acronym for Object-Oriented Design and Analysis, also OODA. Second, as I have read Boyd's works, I have concluded that "plan," as used in the IT context, is closer to Boyd's original meaning than is "deploy."

However, and here is a critical fact, Pete doesn't just do this once. *He does this over and over again.* In fact, Pete is constantly looping through this sequence of OOPA. And, of course, so is his opponent. So who will win? Pete? Or the anti-Pete? If Pete is flying the F-86, we know he will probably win. But why?

It seems that the anti-Pete flying the MiG-15 would be better at OOPA-ing than Pete. Because anti-Pete can see further, he should be able to observe better. Because he can turn and climb faster, he should be able to react faster. Yet the anti-Pete loses and Pete wins.

Boyd decided that the primary determinant to winning dogfights was not observing, orienting, planning, or acting better. The primary determinant to winning dogfights was observing, orienting, planning, and acting faster. In other words, how quickly one could iterate. *Speed of iteration*, Boyd suggested, beats *quality of iteration*.

The next question Boyd asked is this: why would the F-86 iterate faster? The reason, he concluded, was something that nobody had thought was particularly important. It was the fact that the F-86 had a hydraulic flight stick whereas the MiG-15 had a manual flight stick.

Without hydraulics, it took slightly more physical energy to move the MiG-15 flight stick than it did the F-86 flight stick. Even though the MiG-15 would turn faster (or climb higher) once the stick was moved, the amount of energy it took to move the stick was slightly greater for the MiG-15 pilot.

With each iteration, the MiG-15 pilot grew a little more fatigued than the F-86 pilot. And as he gets more fatigued, it took just a bit little longer to complete his OOPA loop. The MiG-15 pilot didn't lose because he got outfought. He lost because he got out-OOPAed.

I'll state Boyd's discovery as Boyd's Law of Iteration: In implementing complex systems, it is better to act quickly than perfectly.

Boyd's law does not mean that you should act carelessly. You can be sure Boyd's pilots were being very careful in every step of their iteration. It's just that they were moving through the iterations as quickly as possible. They were able to do this because their planes were designed (unknowingly, it turns out) to facilitate a crucial step of the iteration, the movement of the flight stick.

Applied to enterprise architectures, Boyd's law tells us that we are going to be better off iterating through our partitions quickly rather than delivering all or most of the partitions in a big-bang way.

In the daily world, I see many situations in which iterative delivery wins over big-bang delivery.

For example, most of us do not buy our dream house as our first house. We buy a modest home that serves to get us into the housing market. The house isn't perfect, but it is good enough. Then, perhaps five years later, we buy a larger house. For many people, the dream house might not be purchased until retirement. This is an iterative approach to housing.

We do not teach children to read by starting them with Shakespeare. Our children start to read by watching Sesame Street. They learn letters, numbers, simple words, phonetics. Then they read very short books (for example, Goodnight Moon), then longer books (for example, Dr. Seuss), then short novels (for example, Charlotte's Web). They build up to Shakespeare. This is an iterative approach to education.

Sometimes you get to watch an organization use both iterative and big-bang approaches. As one such example, consider Starbucks. My longtime readers know that I spend a lot of time at Starbucks. That is where I do most of my writing. That is where I am right now, as I write this. I always get the same thing: doppio macchiatos, one raw sugar, extra foam, no milk, preheat the cup. I have probably drunk thousands of doppio macchiatos at Starbucks. This, I believe, qualifies me as one of the world's leading experts in the Starbucks business model.

Starbucks does a great job with the iterative model. They build a store here, build a store there, and before you know it, Starbucks is everywhere. I have drunk my doppio macchiato every place from the sleepy little town of Brenham, Texas, to the Forbidden City in Beijing. I have never seen a Starbucks location fail. Starbucks is a living testament to the value of the iterative model.

But I have also watched Starbucks attempt to use the big-bang model on three different occasions, and each time resulted in failure.

In 1999, Starbucks, in partnership with Time, introduced a glossy magazine called *Joe*. They built their business case, developed the magazine, and started selling the magazine nationally in Starbucks stores (maybe internationally, I don't know.) Somebody at Starbucks headquarters must have decided that if people would spend five dollars for a coffee, they would also spend five dollars for a magazine about coffee. So overnight, *Joe* was everyplace. This is a big-bang approach. Take your plan and deliver it all at once.

The magazine lasted three issues before, one day, it just disappeared. Starbucks and Time must have lost many tens of millions of dollars on this venture. *Joe* was no more.

In 2004, Starbucks decided to move into chocolate. Suddenly, their menu featured all kinds of exotic (and expensive) hot and cold chocolate drinks to rival their exotic (and expensive) coffee drinks. They put chocolate stands next to their coffee stands. They had promotional material explaining that cocoa beans grew in the shade of coffee beans and therefore if you like coffee, you would like chocolate. (I know, I didn't follow the logic either.)

This new concept was introduced internationally. This effort lasted at most one year, and then, one day, it faded away as quickly as it appeared. Chocolate went the way of Joe. Big-bang delivery and big-bang failure.

In 2005, I watched as Starbucks tried to get into the music business. Starbucks had experienced modest success selling music CDs in their stores. Somebody at Starbucks decided that this was a harbinger for Starbucks to branch out into big-time music sales.

So Starbucks, probably in partnership with HP, created a music kiosk. Each kiosk had four headphones with which you could listen to any of thousands of CDs. You could choose any collection of songs you wanted from those CDs and burn a custom-designed CD for about one dollar per song.

These music stands were introduced at least regionally. Within six months of their introduction, most of the Starbucks I frequented in Texas had these kiosks.

This effort must have been expensive. Not only was there the huge cost of the kiosks, there was the negotiations with the music industry, the cost of installing the kiosks in their stores, the IT costs of managing the whole system. These costs were borne not only by Starbucks, but by their partners as well.

Big-bang, all the way. And, once again, big-bang failure. Within 18 months of the introduction of these kiosks, the last of the kiosks had been removed. Towards the end of their tenure, most of these kiosks were serving as little more than expensive coffee tables.

If Starbucks is any example, you have a much better chance of succeeding with iteration than you do with big-bang delivery. It seems that Starbucks, one of the poster children for iteration, is still learning Boyd's Law the hard way.

Summary

As we look at the world of complexity around us, we notice three fundamental strategies that are used over and over to reduce complexity. These are *partitioning*, *simplification*, and *iteration*.

Partitioning has to do with separating large collections of things into independent subsets, each containing smaller numbers of things. This strategy has a tremendous effect on managing complexity. We will see just how much of an effect in the next chapter.

Simplification is the formal process of taking those subsets and further reducing their complexity by either removing items from the subsets or eliminating entire subsets.

Iteration is the process of rolling those subsets out one by one rather than rolling out the entire collection at once.

Partitioning, simplification, and iteration are concepts that you run into on a daily basis. Once you understand them, they are everywhere. Your local school separates children by grade (partitioning). Your small town newspaper covers only local news (simplification). You plan your summer vacation in stages (iteration). So if these strategies work so well in managing complexity in our everyday lives, why don't we use these same strategies more successfully in enterprise architectures?

That is the question this book has set out to answer.

Chapter 3
Mathematics of Complexity

The last chapter gave an informal introduction to the concept of complexity and to some approaches that we use in our daily lives to control complexity. In this chapter, I am going to take these informal concepts to the next level. I am going to develop a mathematical model for complexity, a model which will then serve as a foundation for a process for developing an enterprise architecture.

In many ways, this approach to enterprise architectures is analogous to the approach currently used with relational databases. Up until 1970, databases were mostly network-like (records contained pointers to records, which contained pointers to records). The network model had no mathematical, logical, or other formal foundation. Without such formality, designing network-like databases was best described as an *irrational* process (or, if you prefer, *nonrational* process). Design was guided by gut feeling, experience, and intuition. An aspiring database architect could not learn *to* design, he or she could only learn *by* designing. I call this approach irrational, because there is no rational (logical and reproducible) methodology that one can learn to follow and there is no way to validate whether a given database design is good or bad other than by building it.

Then in 1970, Edgar Codd of IBM published a paper titled, "A Relational Model for Large Shared Data Banks," in *Communications of the ACM*. This paper presented a mathematical model for databases (*relational* is the mathematical term for tables) and for validating whether or not the data was well organized (the concept of *data normalization*). This mathematical model gave birth to the relational databases that are today ubiquitous. Even though many of today's users of relational databases have little or no idea of the relational mathematical model on which they depend, they still benefit from the formalism that that model provides.

Today is 1970 for the field of enterprise architectures. We have multiple methodologies for designing enterprise architectures (just as we had multiple database design methodologies back in 1970). All of these methodologies are essentially irrational. They rely not on mathematics or logic (the two anchors of the rational world); instead, they rely on experience, gut feeling, intuition, luck, and a host of other intangibles that inhabit the irrational world. Irrational processes sometimes produce successful results, but they often do not. In any case, the results are never reproducible and are never verifiable.

I hope that this chapter will help remedy this situation. It provides a formal mathematical model for understanding complexity, how that complexity manifests itself in enterprise architectures, and what approaches one can use to control that complexity. Because the enterprise architectural process that we will eventually be exploring is grounded in this mathematical model, it is also grounded in the world of the rational. This fact is important because the rational world promises reproducible and verifiable results.

Can we successfully deliver on these promises of delivering reproducible and verifiable results? This chapter is the starting point on your journey to answering this question.

Looking at Complexity

Imagine a software system that monitors penny tosses. It is connected to a box with a sensor at the bottom that relays a message to the software telling it whether the coin lands heads up or tails up. The software system reads the sensor and displays a message on your screen: "Penny is heads" if the penny is heads up, and "Penny is tails" if the coin is tails up. This system is shown in Figure 3-1.

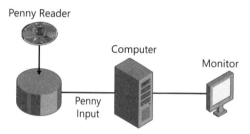

FIGURE 3-1 Penny-toss system.

The software system might look something like the following:

```
values (heads, tails) penny;
penny = read (penny_sensor);
if (penny = heads) message ("Penny is heads");
if (penny = tails) message ("Penny is tails");
end;
```

Suppose that we wanted to prove that the program works for every possible state in which it might find itself. Assuming the hardware works as advertised, how many tests would we need to run to convince ourselves that the program works as well?

We would need to run two tests. The first test would be to drop a penny in the box that lands heads up. If the message came up, "Penny is heads," that test would pass. If the message came up, "Penny is tails" or "Unknown Value," that test would fail. Then we would repeat this test with a coin dropped in the box that lands tails up. Should either test fail, we would say that the system as a whole failed.

Suppose we wanted to validate the software system through code inspection. Most of the lines of code are pretty bland. Actually, only two lines of code require any intellectual effort—the two *if* statements.

If you were to count every possible state in which this program could find itself, you would find that there are two. The first state is the state in which the penny variable is set to *heads*. The second state is the state in which the penny variable is set to *tails*.

Let's say that you are not a technical person. Suppose you want to create a business process to read the flipped penny and generate a memo describing its outcome. This business process might look something like Figure 3-2.

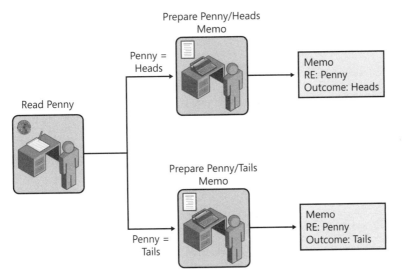

FIGURE 3-2 Business process for examining penny tosses.

Notice that in the penny-toss business process, there is one decision point, and that decision point has two possible paths: one that is followed when the penny comes up *heads*; the other when it comes up *tails*.

Notice that the number *two* reappears several times in this discussion. Two is the number of possible outcomes of flipping a penny. Two is the number of states in which a program can find itself when it has one variable that can take either of two values. Two is the number of challenging statements in a program that monitors coin tosses. Two is the total number of paths in a business process that has one decision point and two possible paths from that decision point.

Now let's make the situation a little more interesting. Let's add a dime into the system. This new software system monitors tosses of pennies and dimes, similar to our last system that monitored penny tosses, and is shown in Figure 3-3.

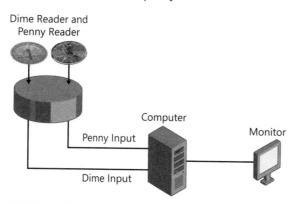

Dime Reader and
Penny Reader

Computer

Monitor

Penny Input

Dime Input

FIGURE 3-3 Penny and dime toss system.

This software system might look something like the following:

```
values (heads, tails) penny, dime;
penny = read (penny_sensor);
dime = read (dime_sensor);
if (penny = heads and dime = heads)
    message ("Penny is heads Dime is heads");
if (penny = heads and dime = tails )
    message ("Penny is heads Dime is tails");
if (penny = tails and dime = tails)
    message ("Penny is tails Dime is tails");
if (penny = tails and dime = heads)
    message ("Penny is tails Dime is heads");
end;
```

Suppose we wanted to prove that this new program works for every possible state in which it might find itself. How many tests would we need to run?

We would need to run four tests—one with the penny landing heads up and the dime heads up; one with the penny landing heads up and the dime tails up; one with the penny landing tails up and the dime heads up; and one with the penny landing tails up and the dime tails up. Four tests.

Suppose we wanted to validate the software system through code inspection. We have four fairly ugly lines of code to look at—the four *if* statements. The remaining lines of code are trivial.

Now let's look at the business process that we might follow for analyzing a penny/dime system. Figure 3-4 shows a business process that would analyze these coin tosses.

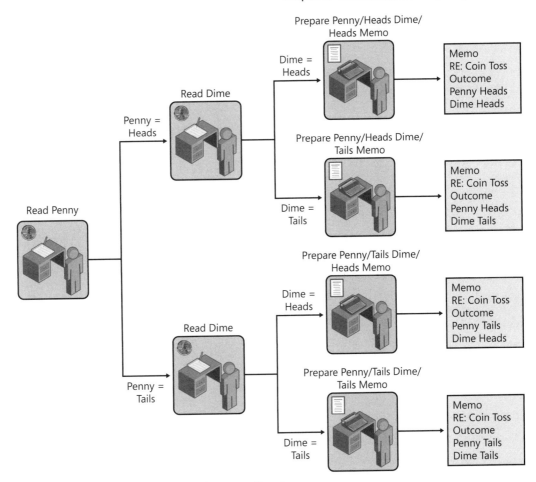

FIGURE 3-4 Business process for examining penny/dime tosses.

Notice that in the penny/dime-toss business process, there are two decision points—one that is based on the state of the penny, and one that is based on the state of the dime. Each of these decision points has two possible paths. The total number of paths that can be traversed within this business process is four. If we wanted to prove to ourselves that this business process works, we would need to examine each of these four paths.

Notice that now the number *four* reappears several times. Four is the number of possible outcomes of flipping a penny and a dime. Four is the number of states in which a program can find itself that has two variables that can each take either of two values. Four is the number of challenging statements in a program that monitors penny-dime tosses. Four is the number of paths in a business process that has two decision points, each with two possible paths.

Laws of Complexity

What is the main contributor to complexity in a software system? I would argue that the number of *system states* is the best measure of complexity. Based on this measure, the penny-dime system (with four system states) is twice as complex as the penny-only system (with two system states). If you compare the two programs, focusing on the *if* statements, you can convince yourself that the second program is roughly twice as complex as the first. It will, for example, take roughly twice as long to analyze for correctness in a code inspection.

This analysis leads to what I shall humbly refer to as Sessions' Law of Software Complexity:

> *The complexity of a software system is a function of the number of states in which that system can find itself.*

A nice thing about Sessions' Law of Complexity is it allows us to make predictions about system complexity even if we can't directly measure system complexity. For example, even if we don't know how complex either of two systems is, we can still measure the relative complexity of the two systems by examining their relative number of states. Because states are often related to variables, states are something that we *can* measure.

The ability to measure relative complexity even without the ability to measure absolute complexity is what I shall refer to as Sessions' First Corollary of Software Complexity:

> *The relative complexity of two software systems—say, system A and system B—is the same as the ratio of the number of states of A divided by the number of states of B.*

So based on the First Corollary of Software Complexity, if we want to compare the penny-only system to the penny-dime system, we can predict that the penny-dime system is twice as complex (the ratio of four states divided by two states). Of course, this answer is the same as we got from our earlier analysis, which is always reassuring.

In general, the number of states in a software system is equal to the number of variables in that system raised to the power of the number of significant states for each variable. So if we have a software system that has two variables, each of which can take on average six significant states, the system as a whole can take on 6^2, or 36, states. So for software systems,

C is the complexity measure

V is the number of variables

S is the number of significant state, on average, for each of the variables

$C = S^V$

Given the First Corollary of Software Complexity, you can now see why the penny-dime program is twice as complex as the penny-only system. The penny-only system has a complexity rating of 2^1, or 2. The penny-dime system has a complexity rating of 2^2, or 4.

Once again, I point out that this complexity analysis does not tell us anything about how complex either program is. We still don't know, for example, if 2 is a low or a high rating for complexity. But what we do know is that however complex the penny-only program is, the penny-dime program is twice as complex.

Now let's return to the business process. What is the main contributor to complexity in a business process? I propose that the number of *paths* is the best measure of complexity. Based on this measure, the penny-dime system (with four paths) is twice as complex as the penny-only system (with two paths). If you compare the two business processes, focusing on the total number of paths, you can convince yourself that the second process is roughly twice as complex as the first. It will, for example, take roughly twice as long in a business process architectural review to inspect the second process than it will take to inspect the first.

In general, the number of paths in a business process is equal to the number of decision points in that process raised to the power of the number of paths (on average) for each decision point. So for a business process that has two decisions points, each of which can take, on average, six paths, the process as a whole has 6^2, or 36, possible paths. So for business processes,

C is the complexity measure

D is the number of decision points

P is the number of paths, on average, for each decision point

$C = P^D$

This analysis leads to the business analogy of Sessions' Law of Software Complexity, which I call Sessions' Law of Business Process Complexity:

> The complexity of a business process is a function of the number of paths possible in the process.

And just as we can for software systems, we can use this law to make predictions about the relative complexity of two different business processes even if we can't directly measure process complexity. We can do this by examining the relative number of possible paths in the two different processes.

This leads to an analogy to the First Corollary of Software Complexity, which I will refer to as the First Corollary of Business Process Complexity:

> The relative complexity of two business processes—say, system A and system B—is equal to the ratio of the number of paths of process A divided by the number of states of process B.

Given the First Corollary of Business Process complexity, you can see why the penny-dime process is twice as complex as the penny-only process. The penny-only process has a complexity rating of 2^1, or 2. The penny-dime process has a complexity rating of 2^2, or 4.

Like the complexity analysis of software systems, this complexity rating does not tell us anything about how complex either process is. We don't know whether 2 is a low or high rating for complexity in processes any more than we knew if it was a low or high rating for complexity in software. But we do know that whatever the complexity of the penny-only process is, the penny-dime process is twice as complex.

Isn't it interesting how similar the two formulas—complexity measurement in software and complexity measurement in business processes—are to each other? Both are of the form

$C = x^z$

There is another system that has a very similar formula for complexity. This is the formula that we use in probability analysis, especially when answering the question how many permutations (for example, outcomes of dice throwing) are there for D distinct dice that each have F faces. The formula is this:

$O = outcomes$

$D = distinct\ dice$

$F = faces\ per\ die$

$O = F^D$

For example, the number of possible outcomes when throwing one die that has two sides (also known as a "coin") is given by 2^1, or 2. The number of possible outcomes when there are two dice that each have two sides (again, coins) is given by 2^2, or 4. Notice the reappearance of those numbers, *two* and *four*.

Homomorphisms

The fact that the mathematics of dice are so similar to the mathematics of software systems and business processes complexity means that we can use mathematical observations about dice permutations to better understand complexity with respect to both software systems and business processes.

Strictly speaking, we describe the relationship between dice systems, software systems, and business processes as *homomorphic*.

A homomorphic relationship is a mathematical relationship between two or more systems in which we can make predictions about one system based on observations of another. A good example of a homomorphic relationship is the relationship between highways and maps. I can predict that Route 1155 intersects Route 290 because

- The line representing 1155 on my map intersects the line representing 290 on my map.
- I believe there is a homomorphic relationship between my map and actual highways.

Controlling Complexity in Dice Systems

The commonality of the complexity function, X^y, establishes a homomorphic relationship between dice and complexity in both software system and business processes. So what can dice teach us about complexity?

Let's start with one six-sided die, and work our way up. A single six-sided die has six possible states in which it can find itself. Any one of these states is equally likely on a given die toss.

A system with two six-sided dice has 36 possible states in which it can find itself, assuming that the dice are individually distinguishable (say, by one being white and the other red). Again, each of these states is equally likely on a given toss.

In general, the number of states of a bucket of dice is a function of both the number of dice and the number of faces on those dice. This formula is

F^D

where F is the number of faces on each die and D is the number of dice. Because F, for six-sided dice, is a constant, 6, this formula reduces to this:

6^D

where D is, still, the number of six-sided dice. Just to do a quick sanity check, when we have 1 six-sided die, this formula tells us we have

$6^D = 6^1 = 6$

or 6 states with one six-sided die. For two six-sided dice, the formula is

$6^D = 6^2 = 36$

or 36 states with two dice.

Let's continue adding dice to the bucket and watch what happens to the bucket complexity (the number of possible states of the bucket). Table 3-1 shows the number of states of the bucket with increasing numbers of six-sided dice.

TABLE 3-1 Number of Bucket States for Different Numbers of Dice

Dice	Bucket States
1	6
2	36
3	216
4	1,296
5	7,776
6	46,656
7	279,936
8	1,679,616
9	10,077,696
10	60,466,176
11	362,797,056
12	2,176,782,336

Table 3-1 shows us that by the time our bucket has reached a mere 12 dice, the number of states has exceeded 2 billion states. Based on this and the homomorphic relationship between dice and software system complexity, we can assume that a program of 12 variables, each of which can take six significant states, would also have in excess of 2 billion possible states.

Also based on this and the homomorphic relationship between dice and business process complexity, we can assume that a business process with 12 decision points, each with six paths, would have in excess of 2 billion possible paths. Clearly, such a program or business process would be very, very complex.

There is another interesting observation we can make about our dice system. If we go from 11 to 12 dice, we increase the number of dice by less than 10 percent. But what happens to the number of states of the bucket? It increases six times.

This tells us something about complexity in software systems and business processes. In either, adding a relatively small increment of functionality often has huge effects on the overall complexity of the system. Most of us in the IT world have seen this phenomenon first-hand, when adding a seemingly small piece of functionality to an existing system breaks the system in ways that could have never been predicted. This is also the reason that so many of us are reticent to install upgrades of existing systems until plenty of others have had the fun of finding all the new problems the new functionality introduces.

Adding Buckets

Let's review where we are. We have discovered that the number of states of 12 six-sided dice is very, very large. Or have we?

Perhaps all we have discovered is that the number of states of 12 dice in a single bucket is very, very large. But what if we divide up the dice into more than one bucket? What if we extend our analysis to not only numbers of dice, but numbers of buckets *and* dice?

Let's take, for example, a system of one bucket and two dice and compare it to a system of two buckets with one die each. The first bucket can now have any of six states. The second bucket can now also have any of six states. These two buckets are shown in Figure 3-5.

1 Bucket/2 Dice   2 Buckets/1 Die Each

FIGURE 3-5 One-bucket and two-bucket systems.

The first bucket contributes six states to the overall system of buckets and dice, as does the second bucket. So all in all, we have a system of 12 states, six from the first bucket and six from the second.

If you have trouble seeing this, think of trying to prove that the buckets are fair—that is, not weighted for or against any one outcome.

In the one-bucket system, you have to throw the dice about 36 times to convince yourself that most outcomes are coming up once and that no outcomes are coming up much more than once. So it takes about 36 throws to convince yourself the system as a whole is fair.

In the two-bucket system, you have to throw the dice in the first bucket about six times to convince yourself that the bucket is fair. Then you have to throw the dice in the second bucket about six times to convince yourself that that bucket is fair. So with 12 throws, you would be reasonably convinced that the system as a whole is fair. By splitting the dice into two buckets, we have reduced by 66 percent the number of dice throws we need to convince ourselves of fairness.

This test of "fairness" is similar to what we would do to convince ourselves that our software systems and/or business processes worked as advertised. Here, instead of throwing dice, we are doing code reviews or path analysis. But the effect of splitting up the system on complexity reduction will be mathematically analogous.

The general formula for the number of states of B buckets, each containing D dice, each of which has F faces, is

$B \times F^D$

For six-sided dice, the formula becomes

$B \times 6^D$

It never hurts to do a sanity check, so let's compare this formula to the results we found earlier with one bucket, or B equal to 1. For one die, we get

$1 \times 6^1 = 6$

For two dice, we get

$1 \times 6^2 = 36$

So far, so good. Our results are consistent. Now let's start playing with the buckets. Let's go back to our bucket of 12 dice. These had over 2 billion states. What happens if we divide the 12 dice into two buckets? Or three buckets? The result, I will tell you right now, is nothing short of breathtaking.

With two buckets of six six-sided dice each, the number of states of our 12-dice system becomes

$2 \times 6^6 = 93,000$

In other words, by dividing the dice into two buckets, we reduce the number of possible states from over 2 billion to just over 90,000. That is a huge reduction in the number of possible states (a 99.99571-percent reduction, to be exact). If we add a third bucket, the number of states of our 12-dice system becomes

$3 \times 4^3 = 3,888$

Figure 3-6 shows visually the difference between the one-, two-, and three-bucket systems.

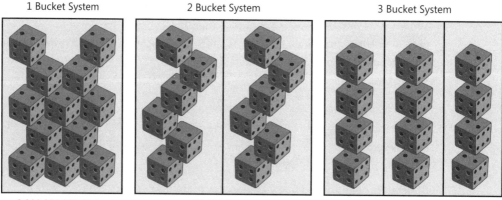

FIGURE 3-6 One-, two-, and three-bucket systems of 12 six-sided dice.

In other words, a system of 12 six-sided dice in one bucket has more than 500,000 times more states than a system of 12 six-sided dice in three buckets. Or equivalently, a system of 12 six-sided dice in three buckets is 0.00000179 as complex as a system of 12 six-sided dice in one bucket. The precise numbers are shown in Table 3-2.

TABLE 3-2 Bucket Complexity with Increasing Buckets (Total 12 Six-Sided Dice)

Buckets	Dice/Bucket	Total States
1	12	2,176,782,336
2	6	93,312
3	4	3,888
4	3	864
6	2	216
12	1	72

This dramatic reduction on overall system complexity seems to me rather amazing, given that we have exactly the same number of dice in both systems, and only a slight increase in the number of buckets (from one to three).

Partitioning

The analysis on state reduction shows that through the splitting of our collection of dice into multiple buckets, we greatly reduce the number of states (and thus, complexity) of the system. But this analysis assumes that each one of the original dice lives in one and only one of the buckets. If we had a die that moved back and forth between the buckets, our analysis would be faulty.

There is a mathematical concept that describes the splitting of a universe of elements (in this case, dice) into two or more groups so that every element lives in one and only one group and does not move from one to the other. This is the concept of *partitioning*. I discussed partitioning informally in the last chapter. Now we will look at a formal definition of partitioning.

A partition is a concept that comes from *set theory*. A partition is a set of subsets that divide a larger set in such a way that all points in the larger set live in one, and only one, of the subsets. Figure 3-7 shows a universe of elements divided into sets of subsets, some of which are true partitions and some of which are not.

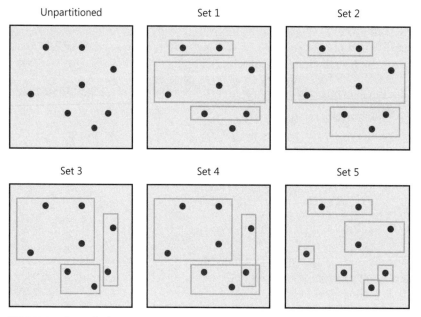

FIGURE 3-7 Sets of subsets.

Looking at Figure 3-7, the box in the upper left (marked *Unpartitioned*) shows a universe of elements. The next five boxes show five different sets of subsets of that universe. Sets 1 through 4 contain three subsets each; Set 5 is a set of six subsets. Set 1 is not a partition because there is one point that is not assigned to any subset. Sets 2, 3, and 5 are all partitions because in each case every point lives in one and only one subset. Set 4 is not a partition, because one point lives in more than one subset.

From the analysis of Figure 3-7, we can also point out an interesting fact about partitions: for a given universe of elements, there are a number of ways to create valid partitions. How many? The math is a bit more complex than is worth going into, but suffice it to say that if there are N elements in the original universe, there are at least N possible ways to partition that universe, and as N increases to meaningful values, the number of partitions increases rapidly.

Once our dice are split into buckets, each die lives in one, and only one, bucket. Therefore, the buckets can be described as a partition of the dice. Based on our state analysis of dice buckets, we can now say that a partitioned system of dice is going to have fewer states than an unpartitioned system of dice. How many fewer? It depends on how many dice we started out with and how many dice ended up in each subset of the partition. But potentially, the partitioned system of dice can have a lot fewer states. Perhaps a whole lot fewer.

So to simplify systems of dice, all we need to do is partition them. And because dice represent complexity in business processes and software systems, we can conclude that by partitioning those systems, we can also greatly reduce their complexity.

This sounds simple, doesn't it? Just split up the 12 dice into two subsets that form a partition! For dice, this might work, but what about variables and paths? Remember, these dice represent variables in software systems and paths in business processes. Ultimately, it is their complexity with which we are concerned.

In software systems, it isn't enough to partition the variables into different subsets. There are a large number of potential partitions. We need to find one that honors dependencies between the variables. How do we know which of these multiple partitions honors the dependencies?

Similarly, in business processes, it isn't enough to partition the decision points into different subsets. Like their cousins, the software systems, there are a large number of potential subsets, and we must find one that honors dependencies between them. How do we know which of the many partitions honors these dependencies?

Equivalence Relations

There is a mathematical property of partitions that can help us here. Mathematically, partitions are closely related to a concept called *equivalence relations*. An equivalence relation (E) is a Boolean (true/false) binary (two-member) relation over some universe of elements such that for any elements—say, a, b, and c—the following three properties are always true:

- E(a, a) is always true—known as the property of *reflexivity*
- E(a, b) always implies E(b, a)—known as the property of *symmetry*
- E(a, b) and E(b, c) always implies E(a, c)—known as the property of *transitivity*

Consider a small store. We can think of all the items in a store as being a particular universe. The relation *costs the same as* is an equivalence relation. Let's say the store currently stocks the 10 items shown in Table 3-3.

TABLE 3-3 Items for Sale in a Small Store

Item	Category	Cost
Cereal	Food	$1.00
Notebook	Stationery	$2.00
Pencil	Stationery	$.50
Pen	Stationery	$1.00
Candy	Food	$.75
Flour	Food	$2.00
Newspaper	Reading	$.50
Soda	Food	$1.00
Cup	Housewares	$2.00
Knife	Housewares	$5.00

Here are some *true* relationships based on the *cost the same as* equivalence relations:

costs the same as (cereal, pen)

costs the same as (notebook, flour)

Here are some *false* relationships based on the *cost the same as* equivalence relations:

costs the same as (cereal, pencil)

costs the same as (candy, newspaper)

Notice that the three equivalence relation properties hold true for the *cost the same as* relation:

costs the same as (cereal, cereal) = reflexivity

costs the same as (cereal, pen) implies *costs the same as (pen, cereal)* = symmetry

costs the same as (cereal, pen) and *costs the same as (pen, soda)* implies *costs the same as (cereal, soda)* = transitivity

These three properties, of course, are true for all elements of the universe of store items. I have just chosen some representative elements to illustrate the properties.

What makes equivalence relations interesting from the perspective of partitioning is that equivalence relations can be used to manufacture partitions. For example, if we create subsets of our store items for which the *costs the same as* equivalence relation is true, we get the following subsets:

Subset 1: cereal, pen, soda

Subset 2: notebook, flour, cup

Subset 3: pencil, newspaper

Subset 4: candy

Subset 5: knife

The name of these subsets (for example, Subset 1) is arbitrary. There is no reason we can't give them names that reflect the relationship between elements of the subset—in which case, we get the more comfortable looking

Items that cost $1.00: cereal, pen, soda

Items that cost $2.00: notebook, flour, cup

Items that cost $0.50: pencil, newspaper

Items that cost $0.75: candy

Items that cost $5.00: knife

Because every element of our original universe lives in one, and only one, subset, these five subsets form a valid partition. Thus, we can use *equivalence relations* to manufacture *partitions*.

Just to make sure we are clear on the concept, let's go through the algorithm for creating partitions from equivalence relations. Here is the algorithm for any equivalence relation, say *E*:

1. Pick one of the elements that has not yet been assigned a subset. Let's call this element e1.

2. Choose one of the subsets from the set of subsets. Let's call this subset S1.

3. Choose one random element from S1. Let's call this r1.

4. Check E(e1, r1).

5. If the result is TRUE, assign e1 to S1.

6. If the result is FALSE, start again at step 2 with another subset.

7. If you exhaust all the subsets without finding a home for e1, create a new subset and assign e1 to that new subset.

8. Continue with step 1 until all the unassigned elements have been exhausted.

Let's follow this algorithm through with the universe of items in our hypothetical store and the equivalence relation *costs the same as,* which I will abbreviate as *C*.

First, what is our universe of elements? It is the items available for sale—namely, cereal, note-book, pencil, pen, candy, flour, newspaper, soda, cup, and knife. Step 1 says that we should choose a random element. Let's choose *pen*.

For our first time through, there are no subsets in the set of subsets, so we skip down to step 7. This tells us to create a new subset and assign *pen* to that subset. We might as well give that subset a name while we are at it. Let's call it *items that cost $1.00*. Now we start again with step 1.

We choose another item, say, *pencil*. I notice that *pencil* seems kind of like a pen, maybe it will end up in the same subset. Let's follow the algorithm.

Step 2 says choose one of the subsets. At this point, we only have one subset, and this is the subset that we named *items that cost $1.00*.

Step 3 says choose a random element from that subset. We only have one element in the subset, and that is *pen*. So what the heck, choose *pen*.

Step 4 tells us to test C (pencil, pen). What do we get? We get false. Why? Because pens cost $1.00 and pencils cost $0.50.

At this point, we have exhausted our subsets, so step 7 tells us to create a new subset and assign pencil to that subset. What shall we call that subset? I have an idea! Let's call it *items that cost $0.50*!

Notice that *cost the same as* is not the only equivalence relation we could have looked at. Another equivalence relation is *same category as*. How do we know that *same category as* is also an equivalence relation? All we need do is test the relation against the three equivalence relation properties: reflexivity, symmetry, and transitivity.

Every item is the same category as itself. Cereal, for example, has the category of food, and this is the same category as cereal. Thus, reflexivity exists. If cereal is the same category as flour, flour must be in the same category as cereal. Thus, symmetry exists. If cereal is the same category as flour and flour is the same category as candy, then cereal must also be the same category as candy (hard to believe, I know!). And that means, we have transitivity, too. So *same category as* is an equivalence relation.

And, like any equivalence relation, it too can be used to manufacture partitions. If we use the *same category as* equivalence relation to manufacture partitions, we get these partitions:

food: cereal, candy, flour, soda

stationery: notebook, pencil, pen

reading: newspaper

housewares: cup, knife

Just like the partition manufactured from the equivalence relation *cost the same as*, this partition is a true partition. Every item lives in one, and only one, subset. The subsets look different than the ones constructed from *costs the same as*, but the subsets are a valid partition, nevertheless.

This leads us to an interesting fact: while there are many valid partitions for a particular universe, there is one, and only one, partition that results from the application of a particular equivalence relation on that universe. A given universe and a given equivalence relation results in a completely unique partition of subsets. As we shall see, when it comes to partitioning enterprise architectures, this property becomes very important.

Not only is the partition created by applying an equivalence relation to a universe unique, it is reproducible. You can apply the equivalence relation 10 times to the same universe, and you will always get exactly the same partition. You can bring in 10 different people, even people who know nothing about partitioning, teach them the equivalence-relation algorithm and every one of them will come up with exactly the same partition.

In fact, they don't even need to know anything about equivalence relations. If you have a black box that returns yes or no depending on whether a given equivalence relation is true or false for two elements of the universe, any person can use this box to create the partitions knowing nothing whatsoever about how the box made its determination. This person would create exactly the same partition as one who had spent a lifetime studying the mathematics of partitions.

The reproducible nature of equivalence relations is important when we apply these concepts to enterprise architectures. Recall that one of my criticisms of existing approaches (for example, TOGAF or Zachman) is that they are not reproducible. If you have two different teams of architects analyzing the same problem, they will likely come up with very different solutions.

But when we use partitioning as a way of organizing our enterprise architecture and use equivalence relations to create those partitions, suddenly the enterprise architecture is largely reproducible. Two different teams of architects analyzing the same problem will likely come up with solutions that, while perhaps not identical, are very similar.

Equivalence Classes

The language of partitions can get a bit awkward. We end up using statements like, "If A and B live in the same subset of a set of subsets that collectively form a partition." It's pretty easy to get lost in the semantics. So I'll introduce another mathematical term that can serve as a shorthand way of expressing that statement.

When an equivalence relation is used to generate a partition, we of course end up with a set of subsets that collectively form a partition. Any one of those subsets contains a bunch of elements that are all "equivalent" to each other—in the sense that you can take any two of them, apply the equivalence relationship to them, and be confident that it will return TRUE. It doesn't matter which two elements you choose or which subset you choose them from. It matters only that the elements come from the same subset.

All the elements in a given subset are therefore related, or equivalent, to each other, with respect to a particular equivalence relation. They are all in the same "class," if *class* is defined as elements that all are equivalent to each other. So rather than say that two elements are in the same subset of a set of subsets that collectively make up a partition (you can see why we don't want to say this), I will just say that the two elements are in the same equivalence class. It means the same thing.

Strictly speaking, we should say that they are in the same equivalence class with respect to a particular equivalence relation, but usually we know which equivalence relation we are talking about.

Inverse Equivalence Relations

There is another type of Boolean binary relation that, while not an equivalence relation, is interesting in its own right. This is an *inverse equivalence relation*. An inverse equivalence relation is the opposite of an equivalence relation. Whenever the equivalence relation is TRUE, the inverse of that equivalence relation is FALSE, and vice versa.

The inverse of an equivalence relation is never itself an equivalence relation. You can see this if you think about the *doesn't cost the same as* relation, which is the inverse of the *costs the same as* equivalence relation. Check the reflexive property, for example. This property is never true for an inverse equivalence relation. Notice that *doesn't cost the same as (cereal, cereal)* is always false, as it is for all other elements of the universe.

Transitivity, is also not a property of *doesn't cost the same as*. The relation *doesn't cost the same as* is true for the pair *cereal* and *pencil,* and also true for the pair *pencil* and *soda*. But the relation is not true for *cereal* and *soda*. Thus, transitivity does not hold. Because neither reflexivity nor transitivity holds for *doesn't cost the same as*, it is not an equivalence relation.

Although the inverse of an equivalence relation is never itself an equivalence relation (and therefore cannot be used as a basis for partitioning), the fact that it is an inverse of an equivalence relation gives it some interesting mathematical properties of its own.

Let's denote an inverse equivalence relation of an equivalence relation E as ~*E*. If E was used to generate the partition, the following two statements can be made about any two elements of the universe, say a and b:

1. If a and b are in the same equivalence class of E, then ~E(a,b) is always false.

2. If a and b are in different equivalence classes of E, then ~E(a,b) is always true.

I will call this combination of two properties *nonequivalence*.

This might all sound terribly confusing, but let's go back to the store example. If we have the set of subsets generated using the equivalence relation *costs the same as*, the *doesn't cost the same as* relation is false for any two elements in the same equivalence class (for example, the equivalence class *items that cost $1.00*) and true for any two elements in different equivalence classes. In other words, *doesn't cost the same as* has the property of nonequivalence.

This leads you to a useful trick. Let's say you want to generate a partition of subsets such that for some Boolean binary relation—say, *R*—the property of nonequivalence holds. How would you go about constructing such a partition?

Try it, for example, with the universe of store elements and the relation *doesn't cost the same as*. Tell me the algorithm you will use to assign each element to subsets so that *doesn't cost the same as* is false for all elements within a subset and true for all elements across subsets. It isn't easy, is it?

But once you realize that *doesn't cost the same as* is an inverse equivalence relation and that the equivalence relation is the inverse of is *costs the same as*, the exercise becomes trivial. Just construct the subsets using the equivalence relation *costs the same as* (we already know how to do that), and you will automatically have the property of nonequivalence for the relation *doesn't cost the same as*.

It's like magic, isn't it?

Now, let's go back to our earlier problem—how to split up our 12 dice into a partition of 2 (or more) subsets. Remember that the dice are homomorphically related to variables (in software systems) and paths (in business processes). And recall, also, that while dice might not have much of an opinion as to which subset they end up in, variables and paths are a little more fussy. Split them up wrong, and the underlying systems no longer function. Split them up correctly, and not only do the underlying systems still work, but their overall complexity has just been dramatically reduced. A payoff like that is worth a little effort.

For software systems, we can create our simplified partitions if we can find an equivalence relation on the variables. Any equivalence relation will do as far as creating a valid partition, but we would like one that specifically preserves logical dependencies between the variables.

For business processes, we can create our simplified partitions if we can find an equivalence relation on the decision points. Again, any equivalence relation will do as far as creating a valid partition is concerned, but we want one that specifically preserves logical dependencies between the decision points.

Equivalence Relations and Enterprise Architectures

That brings us back to enterprise architectures. In our approach to partitioning enterprise architectures, we will seek an equivalence relation not on the variables (for software systems) or decision points (for business processes), but, rather, on the *functionality* of the overall enterprise architecture. Because the enterprise architecture includes both the IT and business architecture (at least, as I define it), any partitioning of functionality of the enterprise architecture will necessarily partition both the IT and business systems that enterprise architecture contains.

Functionality indirectly controls variables on the software side and decision points on the business process side. Adding functionality to a system typically adds both variables to the underlying software systems and decision points to the underlying business processes. Partitioning *functionality* at the enterprise architecture level effectively partitions both the underlying related variables, on the software side, and the underlying related decision points, on the business process side.

So we will focus not on equivalence relations on variables (which are really implementation details that live at the software application architecture level) or equivalence relations on decision points (which are really implementation details that live at the business architecture level). Instead, we will focus on equivalence relations on *functionality.*

The equivalence relation in the enterprise architecture space that is of most interest to us is synergy. Two functions are *synergistic* when each requires the other to be effective—when you can't imagine a situation when one of the functions would be used and the other wouldn't be used. The inverse of synergistic is *autonomous.* Two functions are autonomous when you can imagine situations in which one would be used and the other wouldn't be used.

Let's consider some examples of the universe of functionality that we might encounter in creating an enterprise architecture for a retail operation. Some possibilities are

calculate total cost

calculate change

charge credit card

remove from inventory

report on current inventory

Applying the *synergy* test to this universe, we can see that *calculating total cost* is synergistic with *calculate change.* It's hard to imagine either without the other.

At first glance, it might appear that *charge credit card* is also synergistic with *calculate total cost,* because you can't charge a credit card without knowing the total cost. However, *synergy* is a two-way street—it requires *mutual* dependency (the property of *symmetry*). It is possible to imagine situations where you would want to calculate the total cost without charging credit cards (in a cash-only transaction, for example). Therefore, *charge credit card* is not considered synergistic with *calculate change.* Rather, the two are considered *autonomous.*

It is easy to show that synergy, as defined here, is an equivalence relation, because it satisfies the three properties of equivalence relations (reflexivity, symmetry, and transitivity). Therefore, it, like all equivalence relations, also defines a *partition* of our universe. And further, it defines not only a partition, but a *unique* partition. And not only a unique partition, but a *reproducible* partition. There is only one system of partitioning that can result from applying this (or any) equivalence relation, and you will get the same partition no matter how often you go through the exercise.

Whereas *synergistic* is an equivalence relation and therefore can be used to define a valid partition, *autonomous*—its inverse—is not an equivalence relation. As I have discussed, the inverse of an equivalence relation is never an equivalence relation.

Why is all of this important? Well, it turns out that in enterprise architectures, *synergistic* is not a particularly important property. On the other hand, *autonomy* is a very important property. The best possible partition of an enterprise architecture is one in which the elements in any one subset are autonomous with respect to the elements in any other subset and not autonomous (or, as we might say, synergistic) with respect to each other. Does this sound familiar? This is the property of nonequivalence that I discussed earlier.

But how to assign elements to subsets so that within a subset they are *not* autonomous and across subsets they *are* autonomous is not obvious. What to do? The relationship between equivalence relations and inverse equivalence relations comes to our rescue. When we use an equivalence relation to generate a partition of subsets, those subsets will always have the property of nonequivalence for the inverse of the generating equivalence relation.

So to create a partition of subsets such that nonequivalence—with respect to *autonomy*—is true, we just need to show that the partition was generated with the equivalence function of which autonomy is its inverse. What relation is that? Synergy!

The ideal way to partition a universe of enterprise architectural functionality is such that any two elements of functionality that end up in the same equivalence class are not autonomous (or, are synergistic) with respect to each other and any two elements of functionality that ended up in different equivalence classes are autonomous with respect to each other. This is an incredibly useful way of partitioning an enterprise architecture. It maps well to the eventual goal of generating such technical architectures as service-oriented architectures and hosted services architectures.

And not only is this an incredibly *useful* way to partition an enterprise architecture, it is actually *the best possible* way to partition the enterprise architecture! Why is it the best possible way to partition the architecture? Because if we used any smaller subsets, we would actually add complexity to resolve functional dependencies across subsets. Any larger subsets would give us unnecessary complexity due to bloated subsets. So synergy/autonomy strikes the ideal balance in which subsets are as small as possible, but no smaller. Or, to quote Albert Einstein, we have made the world as simple as possible, but no simpler.

This is a very important result: applying the synergistic equivalence relation against a universe of enterprise architectural functionality yields the *best possible partition* of that universe based on the criteria of complexity. Not because we care that much about synergy, but because we care a lot about autonomy. Autonomy is critical to controlling complexity. And controlling complexity, you might recall, is job number one.

Even without understanding much about my particular enterprise architectural process, you can see applications for this theory. For example, in the area of service-oriented architectures, you often hear the term *autonomous* bandied about with reckless abandon. Services, you will hear, should be autonomous from each other. But what does that mean? How do you know if you have it? Most people couldn't tell you. But now you are starting to see a mathematically based approach to answering that question.

Synergistic in Practice

You don't have enough information yet to know how you would apply this model to enterprise architectures, but you can guess that it has to do with applying the synergistic equivalence relation to the universe of enterprise functionality. In fact, deciding whether functions *are* and *are not* synergistic is, in my approach, the critical architectural decision. There are a number of advantages to this focus on synergy that I have seen in practice.

The first is that the focus on synergy dramatically reduces the number of debates that occur in creating an enterprise architecture. Nothing will completely eliminate debates (we are dealing with architects, after all!), but Simple Iterative Partitions (SIP) greatly reduces the number of topics that are open for debate.

For example, I was recently working with a large consulting organization to begin the process of partitioning its enterprise. Because we had agreed to use synergy-based partitioning, we had no debates about database record format, technological preferences, or messaging infrastructure—topics that can often lead to endless (and usually pointless) discussions. Our discussions were focused only on whether specific functions (say, consulting and billing) were synergistic or not. It's not that those other issues (database record format, and so on) won't eventually be addressed, but they can be dealt with in the relatively peaceful world of solution architecture rather than in the chaotic world of enterprise architecture.

Second, debates about synergies tend to focus on important issues. In a recent large government health organization, I was working with two architects. During the time I was with them, the only significant debate had to do with whether functions related to *general practice* were synergistic with functions related to *surgery*. At one point, I stopped the debate and mentioned to them that I suspected that this was probably the first time the two of them had been involved in a debate that was actually relevant to enterprise architecture. Both agreed that was probably true.

Third, debates about synergisms are easier to resolve. If you can't agree on whether two functions are or aren't synergistic, you have a relatively simple topic that you can either escalate or bring to a subject matter expert. So it is unusual to spend hours and hours of unproductive time debating issues, as is common in traditional approaches to enterprise architecture.

Fourth, debates about synergy tend to be collaborative rather than confrontational. I can't explain why this is, but my experience suggests that when it comes to synergies, people tend not to get wrapped up emotionally in the outcome of the debate. Traditional architectural discussions quickly lead to people taking formal positions. Once one has taken a formal position, one becomes ego-invested in the outcome of the debate. Once egos have been invested, it is difficult to move the process forward. And when the process does finally move forward, it is only with some people being "winners" and others being "losers." The winners add to their collection of prestige points; the losers feel like, well, losers; and the importance of whatever decision was made becomes lost amidst the reshuffling of the institutional peck-ing order.

This doesn't seem to happen with discussions about synergisms. "Synergistic" just doesn't engender the same sort of inflexible opinions that so many other architectural topics bring forth. So rather than take hard-and-fast positions, people typically discuss the issue of syn-ergy with considerable give and take. And because discussions about synergisms are the major points of debate in a partition-focused approach to enterprise architecture, this approach tends to be a much more friendly consensus-like process and one in which all participants feel satisfied with and willing to support the outcome.

Removing Faces

Okay, now back to our dice. And keep in mind that dice aren't just dice, they are homomor-phic representatives of variables in software systems and paths in business processes.

Partitioning dice into buckets is not the only way to reduce overall system complexity. While not as dramatic, we can also have an important impact on system complexity by face reduc-tion. By face reduction, I mean reducing the number of faces on a die, say, from six to four.

Recall that the overall formula for system complexity (C) is

$C = B \times F^D$

where B is the number of buckets, F is the number of face on each die, and D is the number of dice in each bucket.

By just looking at the formula, you can see that any reduction in F (face per die) is going to reduce C (system complexity). But again, you might be surprised by how much of a reduction is possible with seemingly slight changes in F.

For example, consider the difference in complexity between two systems—say, A and B. Assume that both systems have one bucket and that the dice in System A have ten faces and the dice in System B have nine faces. I will ignore the practicality of creating physical dice that have nine or ten faces, each with an equal probability of coming up. This is a mind experiment!

When Systems A and B both have one die, the complexity reduction is equal to the face re-duction. The complexity of System A is then

$C_A = B \times F^D = 1 \times 10^1 = 10$

The complexity of System B is

$C_B = B \times F^D = 1 \times 9^1 = 9$

and the relative complexity of B to A is

9/10 = .9

So this analysis shows that when Systems A and B have a single die, the reduction in complexity is the same as the reduction in the number of faces. Both are a 10-percent reduction.

But what happens when we increase the number of dice to two? Now the complexity of System A is

$C_A = B \times F^D = 1 \times 10^2 = 1 \times 10^2 = 100$

and the complexity of System B is

$C_B = B \times F^D = 1 \times 9^2 = 81$

The relative complexity of B to A, when two dice are involved is now

81/100 = .81

This shows us that with a two-dice system, reducing the number of faces by 10 percent (10 faces to 9 faces) has a greater than 10-percent reduction on the overall complexity (a 19-percent reduction in complexity, to be exact).

As you might guess, the more dice you add into the system, the more impact the face reduction has on the overall complexity. For example, if Systems A and B have 20 dice each, the complexity of System A is

$C_A = B \times F^D = 1 \times 10^{20} = 100,000,000,000,000,000,000$

The complexity of System B is

$C_B = B \times F^D = 1 \times 9^{20} = 12,157,665,459,056,900,000$

and the relative complexity of System B to A is

12,157,665,459,056,900,000 / 100,000,000,000,000,000,000 = .12

The net result of this (if you can avoid becoming flummoxed by the large number of digits involved) is that in a 20-dice system, reducing the number of faces from 10 to 9 results in an 87-percent reduction in system complexity. A 10-percent reduction in the number of faces yields an 87-percent reduction in complexity, not a bad return on our investment. But things get even better as we increase the face reduction.

By taking just one more face off of each of our dice, we now have a 20-percent reduction in face number (from 10 to 8). But now the result on overall system complexity is even more marked. With 20 dice, the complexity of System A is still

$C_A = B \times F^D = 1 \times 10^{20} = 100,000,000,000,000,000,000$

But the complexity of System B is now

$C_B = B \times F^D = 1 \times 8^{20} = 1,152,921,504,606,850,000$

The relative complexity of System B to A is

$1,152,921,504,606,850,000 / 100,000,000,000,000,000,000 = .01$

We are now seeing the remarkable result that a seemingly small 20-percent reduction in the number of faces of the dice results in a seeming large 99-percent reduction in the complexity of the system.

If you continue this analysis, you will find that reducing the number of faces per die from ten to five (a 50-percent reduction) will have a 0.999999046 reduction on system complexity!

The result of this analysis shows how important even seemingly insignificant reductions on the number of possible states for elements in a system is. And that the more elements you have in your system, the greater the impact that state reduction has.

How does this relate to enterprise architectures? The homomorphic equivalent of removing faces from dice is either reducing the number of states a variable can take (in the software system) or removing paths emanating from decision points (in a business process). Both of these will occur automatically if we minimize the work responsibilities of each partition. Does *patient management* really need to send out quarterly statements? If not, get rid of it. When you reduce unnecessary functionality, you reduce complexity in the overall enterprise architecture in general and in the software systems and business processes in particular. How do you determine what is unnecessary functionality? We will discuss this more in Chapter 5, "The SIP Process."

Removing Buckets

We have shown that adding buckets to a system has a dramatic impact on system complexity. As I discussed earlier, if System A has 12 six-sided dice in one bucket, the complexity of System A is

$C_A = B \times F^D = 1 \times 6^{12} = 2,176,782,336$

If System B has the same number of six-sided dice in three buckets, its complexity is

$C_B = B \times F^D = 3 \times 6^4 = 3,888$

The resulting complexity reduction is in excess of 99.999 percent. Now let's compare System B, with three buckets of four dice each, to System C, with two buckets of four dice each. In other worlds, System C is System B with one bucket removed. The complexity of System C is

$C_C = B \times F^D = 2 \times 6^4 = 2 \times 1296 = 2592$

The relative complexity of System C to System B is

3888 / 2592 = .67

This shows that by removing one of the three buckets in System B, we reduce its complexity by 33 percent. Although this is not as dramatic a reduction as we have seen in previous approaches, it is still significant.

What is perhaps most interesting about this analysis is the paradoxical result that we can reduce system complexity by either increasing the number of buckets (as we did in going from System A to System B) or by decreasing the number of buckets (as we did in going from System B to System C). How can both of these be true?

The trick is in realizing that when we went from System A to System B, we added buckets but kept the number of dice in the system constant. We thereby reduced the number of dice in each bucket. When we go from System B to System C, we not only removed a bucket, but also the dice in the bucket. Even though we made no change in the number of dice in the remaining buckets, we decreased the number of dice in the system as a whole.

The bottom line is that removing dice is always a good thing, whether you do it in the system as a whole or in individual buckets.

How does this relate to enterprise architectures? The homomorphic equivalent of throwing away dice by the bucketload is eliminating subsets. There are a number of ways we can eliminate subsets, including outright elimination, outsourcing, and subset consolidation. I will discuss this in Chapter 5.

Other Measures of Complexity

There are several other measures of complexity that are sometimes applied to software systems. Two of the most common are Cyclomatic Complexity Measures and Halstead Complexity Measurement.

Cyclomatic complexity is a measure of the number of linear paths that can be taken through a software program, something similar to the way we are looking at complexity in business processes. An *if/else* statement, for example, typically introduces two possible program paths.

Halstead Complexity is based on computational complexity and is driven by measurements on the operators in the program.

Neither of these is in competition with partition analysis, for a number of reasons. First of all, I believe that complexity as measured by the number of states in a software program is likely closely related to both Cyclomatic Complexity and Halstead Complexity. But more importantly, both Cyclomatic and Halstead measurements are intended to be applied only to software programs. We are focusing on reducing the complexity of enterprise architectures. In this realm, neither Cyclomatic nor Halstead measurements are applicable.

Our philosophy is that you must first reduce the complexity at the enterprise architectural level. Once you have done that, you will end up with a partition consisting of a set of subsets that have been maximally simplified. Each of these subsets will end up with one or more business process components and one or more software components.

When developing the software components, it is appropriate to implement those as simply as possible. While it is not my goal (at least, here) to offer any guidance as to how to write good code (although I do have some opinions on how to package that code—which is the topic of Chapter 7, "Guarding the Boundaries: Software Fortresses"), I support the idea of minimizing program paths. Cyclomatic measurements can help you here. I also support reductions in computational complexity. If you like Halstead, feel free to plug that in here.

The bottom line is that this approach is about reducing complexity at the enterprise architecture level. This simplification will trickle down to both the business processes and the software systems. And once you get to those levels, feel free to use Cyclomatic, Halstead, or any other measurements with which you are comfortable, to write the best possible code (or architect the best possible business processes) you can.

Complexity in Theory and in Practice

As you can see from the dice analysis, a complex system can be greatly simplified by partitioning. The complex systems that we care about are not systems of dice, but systems of enterprises, and ultimately the systems of business processes that drive those enterprise and the systems of technology that support those processes. In the dice analysis, we saw complexity reductions of greater than 99.9 percent with relatively little partitioning. Can we expect to see such dramatic numbers when applying these principles to enterprise architectures?

Probably not. These numbers are theoretical maximums that will be dampened by a number of factors in the real world.

For one thing, variables in software systems are usually not completely random with respect to each other, as are the dice. Some pseudo-partitioning might have already been done using, for example, good structured programming approaches or even object-oriented programming (although object-oriented programming also tends to introduce a lot of variables and muddies the waters with polymorphism). So it takes more variables to achieve the same complexity as one would achieve with a smaller number of dice. Fortunately (from the perspective of complexity management), variables in software systems are usually in great abundance.

One other reason that you shouldn't expect to see the high theoretical complexity reductions in the real world is that it is rare that the partitioned subsets of either software systems or business processes are 100-percent independent of each other.

Typically, there will be some interactions between the subsets—say, with message passing if we implement our subsets with service-oriented architectures, or with database sharing if we implement our subsets using a common data layer. And interactions between subsets are the enemy of partitioning. It is *critical*, therefore, to minimize both the number and the complexity of those interactions.

Because these interactions are likely to be most convoluted in the software systems rather than the business processes, we need to be particularly attentive to balancing our need for interoperability *between* software systems with our commitment to controlling complexity *inside* of software systems. This is an issue that is rarely considered in traditional software architectures.

So what is a reasonable expectation for complexity control? Clearly, the maximum reduction predicted from theoretical analysis, 99.9+-percent, is too high. Buy my experience suggests that 90-percent reductions in complexity from modest numbers of partition subsets are entirely reasonable. This augers savings of 90 percent of the cost of building and maintaining those systems.

My numbers are consistent with at least one independent observer. Cynthia Rettig wrote a paper in the *MIT Sloan Management Review* in which she quoted studies showing that every 25-percent increase in the complexity of the problems being solved by software systems increases the complexity of the software systems themselves by 100 percent. In other words, adding 25 percent more functionality doubles the complexity of the software system. If we assume that these numbers are correct (Rettig is from MIT, after all), what would this tell us about partitioning?

> **Note**   The title of Cynthia Rettig's article is, "The Trouble with Enterprise Software," and it can be found in the August 8, 2007 issue of the MIT Sloan Management Review.

Let's assume that we start out with a system that has 100 different functions. Adding 25-percent complexity to this is equivalent to adding another 25 functions to the original 100. Rettig tells us that this 25-percent increase in functionality doubles the complexity, so the software with 125 functions is now twice as complex as the one with 100 functions. Let's follow this system as we add more functions. Table 3-4 shows how this system increases in both functionality and complexity as we continue adding increments of 25-percent functionality.

TABLE 3-4 Increasing Complexity with Increasing Functionality

Starting functions	% increment	New total	Complexity %
100	0.25	125.00	200.00
125.00	0.25	156.25	400.00
156.25	0.25	195.31	800.00
195.31	0.25	244.14	1600.00
244.14	0.25	305.18	3200.00
305.18	0.25	381.47	6400.00
381.47	0.25	476.84	12800.00

Table 3-4 shows that by the time the system has grown from 100 functions to about 300 functions, the complexity has increased by 3200 percent. This means that we would expect the system with 300 functions to be 32 times more complex than the system with 100 functions.

So if we partition a system with 300 functions into three subsets of 100 functions each, we expect the complexity of each subset to be 1/32nd as complex as the original, since each of our subsets has approximately the same functionality as did our original system of 100 functions. Of course, we have three such systems now, so the total complexity is 3/32nd, or approximately 09.4 percent of the original.

Using Rettig's numbers, we therefore expect a 90.6-percent reduction in complexity through the partitioning of an enterprise architecture into just three subsets. This is very much in line with my informal observations of 90-percent reductions in complexity, and not even far off from the theoretical maximums predicted by the dice studies.

So what should you expect? As they say, your mileage may vary. But the tantalizing promise of 90-percent reductions in complexity and therefore cost of IT systems is a figure that nobody can afford to ignore.

Summary

This material has presented the basic mathematical foundations of managing the complexity of enterprise architectures. My premises include the following:

- Complexity of business processes is mostly related to the number of decision points and paths emanating from those decision points.

- Complexity of software systems is mostly related to the number of variables and the number of significant values those variables can take.

- The complexity of both business processes and software systems can be modeled by systems of dice in which the number of dice, the number of faces on the dice, and how the dice are divided into buckets can be varied.

- Partitioning is the single major factor in reducing complexity of dice systems and, by extension, of software systems and business processes.

- Partitioning is closely related to a mathematical concept known as equivalence relations.

- The most important equivalence relation, from the perspective of enterprise architecture, is one called synergy.

- Synergy is closely related to an inverse equivalence relation known as autonomy. And if you think we care a lot about synergy, you should see the emotions autonomy invokes!

Notice that probability analysis does not model every, or even many, aspects of either a software system or a business process. In fact, it models only one particular aspect of either a software system or a business process. What aspect is that? Complexity! Which just happens to be the aspect that we most care about—at least, in the context of this book.

Part II
The Quest for Simplification

Chapter 4
The ABCs of Enterprise Partitions

I have discussed partitions and their role in reducing complexity in the last two chapters—first, with a conceptual overview, and then with a more rigorous mathematical treatment. By now, you should understand that partitioning is fundamental to managing complexity in enterprise architectures.

In the next chapter, I will discuss the process I recommend for creating a "simple" enterprise architecture. Much of this process will be focused on partitioning the enterprise, as you might guess. But what, exactly, does it mean to *partition* an enterprise? What does a subset of the enterprise look like? What aspects of the enterprise do we attempt to capture in the subsets? And perhaps as important, which do we ignore? Are there higher level relationships that we can use to better understand relationships between these subsets? These are the topics I will discuss in this chapter.

I will spend quite a bit of time discussing relationships between the various units of the enterprise. I will show why these relationships are critical to extrapolating knowledge learned from previous projects, discovering unnecessary complexity in this partition, and finding nonobvious opportunities for architectural simplification.

Review of the Mathematics

I'll start by giving a quick review of the key mathematical concepts.

A *partition* is a set of subsets of a universe such that every element of the universe lives in one, and only one, subset. An *equivalence relation* is a Boolean, binary relation that, when applied to the elements of a universe, has the properties of reflexivity, symmetry, and transitivity. Equivalence relations are particularly interesting with respect to partitions because they can be used to generate sets of subsets that form partitions.

When we have a partitioned set of subsets that was generated with some equivalence function, we can refer to a particular subset in the partition as an *equivalence class*. Knowing that we are looking at an equivalence class tells us several important pieces of information about every element—say, *a* and *b*—in the universe:

- If *a* and *b* are in the same equivalence class, they are equivalent to each other, in whatever sense *equivalence* has with respect to the equivalence relation that was used to generate the subset.

- If *a* is in a particular equivalence class and *b* is a member of the same universe as *a*, then *b* is either in the same equivalence class as *a* or it is in some other equivalence class.

- If *a* and *b* are in different equivalence classes, then they are not equivalent to each other, in whatever sense *equivalence* means with respect to the equivalence relation that was used to generate the subset.

- If *a* and *b* are in different equivalence classes, then the inverse of the equivalence relation that was used to generate the equivalence classes will be true when applied to *a* and *b*.

In an enterprise architecture, the equivalence function that is of the most interest is the *synergistic* function. The inverse of that function is the *autonomous* function.

Partitioning the Enterprise

One of our early goals with Simple Iterative Partitions (SIP) is to create a diagrammatic overview of the enterprise. This overview describes the pieces of the enterprise and how those pieces are related to each other. Many methodologies also include a process that involves creating a diagram of the enterprise, but the SIP diagrams differ in several fundamental ways from these others.

One difference is that most methodologies treat business processes independently from technical solutions. So they might have one set of diagrams that show the flow of the business processes and another set of diagrams that show the architecture of the technical solutions. SIP doesn't distinguish between the business processes and the IT systems that support those processes. From SIP's perspective, this difference is a detail that is best dealt with in the implementation phase, a phase with which SIP is relatively unconcerned.

Another difference is that most methodologies focus on diagramming how an organization works—say, how all of the many business processes (for example, hiring an employee, loading a truck) accomplish their goals. SIP focuses on diagramming the functions of the organization, but it does not try to document how those functions are implemented. SIP focuses on what an organization does, not how it does it. For SIP, it is not important how *loading a truck* is implemented. It is only important that there exists a process for loading a truck, and that that process is related in some defined way to *shipping an order*.

A third difference between SIP and other methodologies is that the latter create diagrams or architectural artifacts that are empirical. By empirical, I mean that they reflect the observations and opinions of a specific individual or group. Two different individuals or groups could create quite different architectural diagrams of the same basic function, because each might interpret processes differently, use different levels of detail, or consider different steps in a process more relevant than others. SIP is based on mathematical, logical, and reproducible processes. Thus, two different groups creating SIP diagrams of the same organization should end up with similar-looking diagrams, and it should be possible to adjudicate any differences using a formal rational analysis.

As I mentioned, in SIP we care little about how a function is implemented. It isn't that the implementation isn't important, it is just that it isn't important at the level of an enterprise architecture that SIP considers important. SIP is concerned with reducing the highly complex enterprise down to a series of simpler functions, and then understanding how those functions relate to each other.

The ABCs of Enterprise Equivalence Classes

The starting point for SIP is an autonomous business capability (ABC). An ABC is mathematically an equivalence class, or one of the sets that collectively make up the partition. Thus, the collection of (or set of) ABCs that define the enterprise are mathematically a partition of the enterprise. This means that every business function of the enterprise lives in one and only one ABC.

The ABC packages together all the business processes and software systems that are synergistic with each other. The A in ABC stands for *autonomous*, which means that the functionality of the ABC works independently of the functionality of other ABCs. The B in ABC stands for *business*, which means that the ABC has some well-defined business purpose. The C stands for *capability*, which means that it is capable of producing some effect that is visible from the outside world. An ABC, or autonomous business capability, is thus a unit of the business that functions autonomously from other business units but interacts with those units in well-defined ways. Two examples of ABCs are *Shipping* or *Accounts Payable*. These ABCs both deliver a well-defined business functionality (or capability), but the functionality of *Shipping* is autonomous with respect to the functionality of *Accounts Payable*.

The ABC model greatly simplifies the overall business model for two important reasons. First, the model benefits from the simplicity that naturally results from a partitioning process. Second, the model slashes through implementation issues by looking only at *what* an ABC does, not *how* it does it. Figure 4-1 pictorially represents the ABC concept.

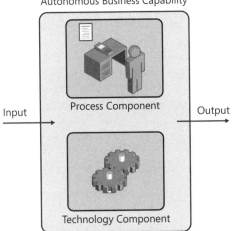

FIGURE 4-1 A prototypical ABC.

Notice that an ABC includes both business process and technology elements. The business process elements describe the process the business follows to do the function defined for the ABC. The technology elements describe the IT functionality that supports those processes. In general, we do not distinguish between the two at the enterprise level. It is enough to know that both are part of the ABC.

ABC-Type Relationships

ABCs can be described by their types, and those types define relationships between ABCs. Before I go too far, let me generate a little enthusiasm for the ability of types to convey informational content.

Consider the three flowers shown in Figure 4-2.

FIGURE 4-2 Three flowers.

Suppose you know something about the first flower (the one on the left), such as whether it likes shade, how it should be fed, and what temperature extremes it can tolerate. What does this tell you about the other two flowers? In general, not much.

But now suppose I tell you something about the types of these flowers. The first and third flowers are both orchids. The middle flower, even though it looks similar to the first flower, is unrelated to orchids. It is actually a Jewelweed (Impatiens capensis). Now you suddenly know two things. The third flower is probably going to respond favorably to similar conditions as the first flower. And the second flower probably won't.

Here is another example. Consider the three chess games shown in Figure 4-3.

FIGURE 4-3 Three chess games.

Suppose I told you that I had exhaustively analyzed the first game (the one on the left). What does this analysis tell me about the second two games? It turns out that the analysis of game 1 tells me nothing whatsoever about game 2. These two games are unrelated. However, there is a close relationship between game 1 and game 3.

It turns out that game 1 and game 3 are not only closely related, they are the same game. The only difference is that the board has been turned around so that rather than viewing the board from white's perspective (game 1) you are now viewing the board from black's perspective (game 3). Even if you don't know much about chess, knowing that you have a good analysis of game 1 and knowing that game 1 is identical to game 3, tells you that the analysis of game 1 is applicable to game 3.

There is a pattern in these examples. Even knowing little about the subject domain itself (flower husbandry and chess rules), you can learn something about one element if you know something about a second element and know how the second element is related to the first.

In general, knowledge about relationships is critical to extrapolating what you know about one thing to other things. Even knowing that two things are *not* related can sometimes carry useful information.

Let's see how these relationships play out in enterprise architectures. Consider Figure 4-4, adapted from a retail client of mine. This figure shows the business architecture as it existed at the time I arrived on the scene. The question was, "Is this a good architecture or a bad architecture?" Take a look at the figure, and try to decide for yourself before continuing.

Before we decide if the architecture is good or not, we need to agree on a definition of *good*. By now, you should know that my definition of *good*, as it relates to architectures, is about complexity. A *good* architecture is one that is as simple as possible while still providing the necessary business functionality. A *bad* architecture is one that is more complex than necessary to deliver the necessary business functionality.

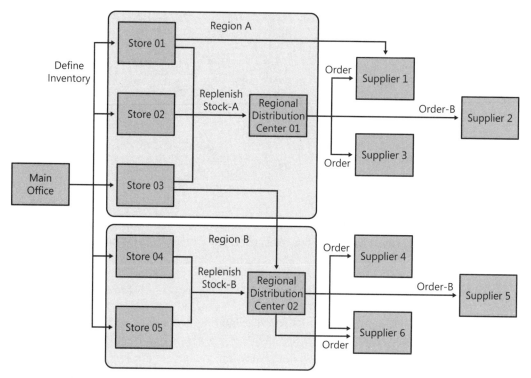

FIGURE 4-4 Retail business architecture.

And simplicity, you also know, is primarily related to partitioning. A well-partitioned architecture is a simple architecture; and if that partitioning is based on the equivalence relation
synergistic, then that architecture is not only simple, it is as simple as it can get.

So does the architecture shown in Figure 4-4 represent an organization in which the enterprise is broken into subsets such that each function lives in one and only one subset? (That is,
is the functionality partitioned?) And are the subsets truly autonomous? (That is, are they as
simple as they can get?)

So how good is the architecture shown in Figure 4-4? The answer is that we don't know. We
have little information that would help us evaluate the architecture with respect to partitioning. We don't know if the functionality of *store 03*, for example, is similar to the functionality
of *store 02*. If it is, the architecture does *not* represent a valid partition (because the store
functionality exists in two subsets, which is a violation of the rules of partitions). If the functionality of store 02 and 03 are "different," our rules of partitioning are intact.

Thus, it becomes very important to be able to determine if the functionality of store 03 and
store 02 are fundamentally the same or fundamentally different, and to do so using a
rational approach. We will use type information to make this determination. Type information
has two useful characteristics. First, it conveys similarities. Second, it is rational.

Implementations and Deployments

Two fundamental type relationships between ABCs are that of *implementation* and *deployment*. Every functioning ABC in an enterprise is a deployment of some ABC implementation.

Let's discuss the difference between ABC implementations and ABC deployments. I'll use as an enterprise example a fictional retail pharmacy that I will call Contoso Pharmaceuticals. Although Contoso is fictional, it is based on a composite of several of my clients.

Contoso has 500 stores in the United States, split into five regions. An ABC deployment is some group of people following a specific process using a specific collection of software functionality. For example, Contoso's Midwest region has a group that manages human resources (HR) for that region. So does the Southwest region. Therefore, both regions have a deployment of a human resources ABC. So, of course, do each of the other three regions, but I will focus on the Southwest and Midwest regions in this discussion.

There are two possibilities as to how the human resource ABC deployments in the two regions are related to each other: with centralized implementation or regional implementation.

In the first case, centralized implementation, the HR business processes are defined by the home office, as are the software systems that support those processes. Both are sent out to the regional offices, which are then responsible for deploying those business processes and software systems.

From an ABC perspective, we describe this approach as two deployments of one human resource implementation. Specifically for Contoso, we can say that we have the Midwest deployment of the Contoso human resource implementation and the Southwest deployment of the Contoso human resource implementation.

I refer to this pattern as *single implementation, multiple deployment*. Because that takes so long to say, I will describe the relationship between two ABC deployments from the same implementation as *clones*.

In the second case, regional implementation, the regional offices are responsible for implementing their own systems. They might have some basic requirements laid down by the home office in terms of reporting accountability, but the regional office is largely on its own for defining and implementing its human resource business processes and supporting software systems.

From an ABC perspective, I describe this approach as two deployments of two different implementations. Specifically for Contoso, we can say that we have the Midwest deployment of the Midwest Contoso human resource implementation. I refer to this pattern as *multiple implementation, multiple deployment*. Again, because that is a mouthful, I will refer to ABC deployments that are from different implementations as ABC *siblings*. I will introduce some more information about the concept of siblings shortly.

As you can see, the second case (siblings) is more complex than the first (clones). In the second case, we have two parallel implementations that do basically the same thing. In fact, we have five parallel implementations, because we can assume the same story is replicated at the other three regions as well. Implementations are typically expensive, and here we are duplicating this expense in each of the five regions.

Why would we want to do this? There are three common histories that result in sibling architectures.

I call the first *parallel evolution*. In parallel evolution, we start with one implementation/multiple deployments—in other words, with a clone architecture. Over time, each region comes up with regionally specific requirements. Because the original implementation doesn't exactly meet the region's needs, the region modifies it slightly to be a better fit. Over time, those modifications accumulate and eventually become effectively a different implementation. At that point, what had started out as a clone architecture has migrated into a sibling architecture. This may happen over long periods of time, and the transition is often not noticed until it is well underway.

Another reason we see sibling architectures is because of what I call *acquisitional redundancy*. In acquisitional redundancy, the different regions were originally entirely different enterprises. Over time, Contoso purchased these independent regions. Each region had its own ways of doing business. For some ABCs, the home office might have dictated the use of centralized ABCs (including both centrally defined processes and centrally created software systems). This scenario most often occurs when dealing with critical business operations, such as, for Contoso, purchasing drugs from wholesalers or submitting claims for insurance reimbursement. In the case of other, less critical, ABCs, the Contoso home office might have decided that the disruption incurred by replacing existing processes and/or systems was not worth the effort. It is possible that HR fits in this latter category.

The third reason we see sibling architectures is *deliberate duplication*. In deliberate duplication, Contoso intentionally decentralizes its operations and allows each region to make its own decisions. Contoso might choose deliberate duplication in the belief that small organizations can be more agile. Contoso might also choose this pattern believing this reduces catastrophic risk, because any given failure can affect only one region.

I have seen at least one organization choose this pattern because it believed that doing so lessened vendor dependency. As you will see in Chapter 6, "A Case Study in Complexity," the organization paid a very heavy price for this decision.

Is it worth migrating sibling architectures to clone architectures? There is no one right answer to this. Arguing against the migration are both the expense and the risk of the migration. Arguing in favor of the migration are the reduction in system complexity and maintenance cost. The question as to whether this project is worth undertaking can be answered only by a formal risk/value analysis, a topic that I will discuss in the next chapter. SIP can prove that an opportunity exists for simplification, but the organization must choose whether or not to pursue the opportunity.

I should also point out that single-implementation/single-deployment ABC systems are quite common but somewhat less interesting from an enterprise architecture perspective, because we have fewer opportunities to simplify them. These are essentially clone systems with only single clones. Still, many highly mission-critical ABCs follow the single clone pattern, and this makes them worthy of our attention. This, and their propensity for turning into sibling systems. We hate to see that.

ABC Types

So implementation and deployment are two types. All ABCs are either an implementation or a deployment. But this is just the start of our type relationships. In addition, we assign every ABC implementation a specific ABC type. This type is a general *category* of ABC, such as human resources. Whereas all deployments are enterprise specific and most implementations are enterprise specific, ABC types tend to be generic across enterprises, especially within the same industry. An ABC type is a generalized description of an ABC, along with some basic information about how ABCs of that category are usually (but not necessarily) implemented.

Actually, we have already used the type concept. In the last section, when I discussed the issue of single-implementation (clone) versus multiple-implementation (sibling), we were using ABC types implicitly. What does it mean for an ABC to follow a multiple-implementation pattern (sibling)? It means that we have multiple implementations for the same *type*. Without types, we cannot recognize the sibling pattern. And this pattern is a critical one from the perspective of simplification through the elimination of whole equivalence classes.

The best way to use types is proactively. We love to hear conversations like the following:

Art: I am going to need a system for managing employees.

Claire: Which of these types best describes this system?

Art: I would say it is an HR system.

Claire: Let me check our inventory. Oh, look, we already have an implementation of an HR system running in our Houston office. Let's see if we can get it modified so that it suits your needs. Wouldn't it be nice if we could get by with a new deployment of that system?

Art: I'll say. That would save me a million dollars or so. Let's check it out.

We need to have some mechanism to show diagrammatically the relationship between deployments, implementations, and ABC types. In my diagrams, I use a solid rectangle to indicate types, a rounded rectangle to indicate implementations, and a dashed-rounded rectangle to indicate deployments. The diagram that describes the clone Contoso HR pattern (abbreviated, showing only two regions) is shown in Figure 4-5, and one describing the sibling Contoso HR pattern (similarly abbreviated) is shown in Figure 4-6. One value in comparing diagrams is that the inefficiencies in the system become more obvious.

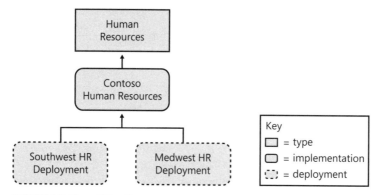

FIGURE 4-5 Clone HR pattern.

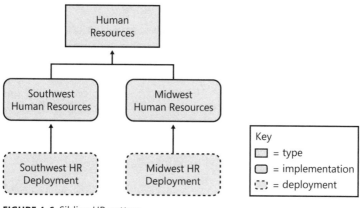

FIGURE 4-6 Sibling HR pattern.

Type Hierarchies

Frequently, we see ABC implementations that seem somewhat related to each other, although not closely enough related to each other that we would describe them as two implementations of the same type (siblings). As an example, Contoso might operate regular retail stores and superstores. Although the implementation of these two ABC types might have overlap, there will also be many differences.

To capture the relationship between ABCs that are similar but not identical, we use the concept of type relationships. We say that *retail store* is one type of ABC, *superstore* is another type of ABC, and they are related to each other by both being specializations of the same ABC type *store*.

Although I have already introduced the term *sibling*, I can now introduce it in a more formal way. I call ABCs that are implementations of the same ABC type *siblings*. In Figure 4-5, the human resource system has only itself as a sibling. In Figure 4-6, the various human resource systems have multiple siblings, one for each region.

I call ABCs that are implementations of ABC types that share a common lineage *cousins*. Implementations of Contoso's *retail store* and *superstore* are cousins of each other because their types are both specializations of *store*. The cousin's relationship can help reduce complexity by identifying ABC implementations that have overlap. If the overlap is strong enough, the implementations are candidates for consolidation. If the overlap is weak, there is still often room for reuse of existing processes and/or software systems.

This notion of type specialization is somewhat analogous to the concept of class hierarchies in object-oriented programming languages, but the ABC types serve only an organizational function. Unlike object classes, ABC types contain no implementation or interface information.

Before I delve into some of the other ABC relationships, let me summarize what I have covered so far:

- The basic unit of an enterprise partition is an *autonomous business capability* (ABC).
- ABCs consist of both business process(es) and IT system(s).
- An actual functioning ABC in the enterprise is a *deployment*.
- All ABC deployments are associated with some ABC *implementation*.
- Ideally, a given ABC implementation has multiple deployments.
- All ABC implementations are associated with an ABC *type*.
- ABC *types* can be either *specializations* or *generalizations* of other ABC types.
- All ABC deployments of the same ABC implementation are known as *clones*.
- All ABC implementations of a given ABC type are known as *siblings*.
- All ABC implementations of ABC types that are both specializations of the same generalized type are known as *cousins*.
- *Cousins* should be investigated for simplification through *reuse*.
- *Siblings* should be investigated for simplification through *consolidation*.
- *Clones* should be put on a pedestal and celebrated.

Composition Relationships

ABCs can be related to each other not only through their types but through compositions of each other. One ABC can be composed of other ABCs or be part of the composition of another ABC. Mathematically, compositions indicate the possibility for further partitioning (and thus, simplification) of an existing equivalence class. So if A is *composed of* B and C, this is to say that A can be broken down into two subsets, B and C, which collectively form a partition of A. Alternatively, we can say that B and C *partition* A.

Compositions can occur in types, implementations, and deployments. In each case, the composition is of the same flavor (type, implementation, or deployment). Composition is interpreted slightly differently in the three flavors.

In the case of types, composition is taken as indicating that implementations of one type are frequently composed of implementations of these other types. So if A, B, and C are all types, and A is composed of B and C, then this is read as saying that A's are frequently implemented through composition of B's and C's. For example, the type *Sales Order Management* is frequently implemented as a composition of the ABC types *Inbound Sales Management* and *Campaign Sales Management*, and thus they can frequently be simplified by partitioning into these types.

In the case of implementations, composition is taken as indicating that this ABC has definitely been implemented through compositional use of these other implementations. So if A, B, and C are all implementations, and A is composed of B and C, then this is read as saying that this implementation of A has been implemented as a composition of this implementation of B and C. For example, *Contoso Sales Order Management* has been implemented as a composition of the ABC implementations *Contoso Inbound Sales Management* and *Contoso Campaign Sales Management*. We can thus simplify the implementation of Contoso Sales Order Management by partitioning it into lower level functions.

In the case of deployments, composition is taken as indicating that this particular deployment has been tied compositionally to these other deployments. So if A, B, and C are all deployments, and A is composed of B and C, then this is read as saying that this deployment of A has been tied compositionally to this deployment of B and C. For example, the deployment of *Southwest District Sales Order Management* has been implemented as a composition of the ABC implementations *Southwest District Inbound Sales Management* and *Southwest District Campaign Sales Management*.

Composition is graphically indicated as a box within an ABC, as shown in Figure 4-7.

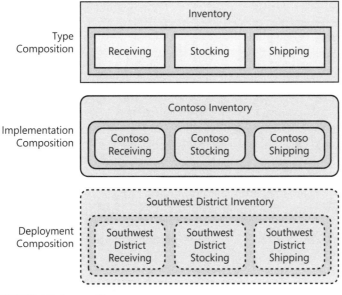

FIGURE 4-7 Composition.

I sometimes call an ABC that is not composed of other ABCs a *terminal* ABC.

Partner Relationships

The final type of relationship that we track for ABCs is *partner relationships*. Partner relationships can be defined at either the type, implementation, or deployment level, but I find they provide the most value at the implementation level.

Two ABCs that have some well-defined interactions are said to be in a *partner relationship*. Partner relationships are shown by connecting implementations by arrows, as shown in Figure 4-8.

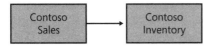

FIGURE 4-8 Partnership.

It is likely that a sales system will want to interact with an inventory system. There will need to be some way for the business processes of sales to interact with the business processes of inventory, and similarly for the two IT systems. Most likely, this interaction will be implemented as interactions between the technology components as shown in Figure 4-9, but this is really an implementation issue for the ABC.

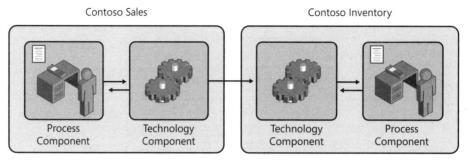

FIGURE 4-9 Typical ABC partner interaction.

When partner relationships are implemented through the technology components, we see three common partner patterns. Referring to Figure 4-9, the patterns are as follows:

1. **Information Request** One ABC—say, the Inventory ABC—requests some information from the other ABC—say, the Sales ABC. An example of such a request might be the daily sales tally.

2. **Information Broadcast** One ABC—say, the Inventory ABC—decides that it has some information that one or more other ABCs—say, the Sales ABCs—need to know about and broadcasts that information to them. An example might be that Inventory has received a new item and lets the Sales ABCs know of the availability of the item.

3. **Work Request** One ABC—say, the Sales ABC—needs the other ABC—say, the Inventory ABC—to do some work. For example, a sale has been made, and the Sales ABC tells Inventory to decrement the item from stock.

You might run into other partner patterns, but in my experience, these three patterns account for a vast number of interactions between ABCs.

Relationships and Partition Simplification

As you can see, there are four very different relationships that ABCs can have with one another. We have implementation/deployment relationships in which ABCs are related to each other based on how many times an implementation is deployed. We have ABC type relationships, in which ABCs are related to each other based on common categories. We have compositional relationships, in which ABCs can be broken down into lower level ABCs or composed up into higher level ABCs. And we have partner relationships, in which we can model interactions between ABCs. Why do we need all these relationships? After all, SIP is supposed to be about simplicity. This doesn't look all that simple!

Remember, SIP approaches complexity control through three key approaches: partitioning, simplification, and iteration. Each of the ABC relationships is oriented toward one or more of these approaches. Let's go through the relationships again and show how they relate to complexity control.

Type relationships are key to identifying equivalence class consolidation opportunities. Recall from Chapter 3, "Mathematics of Complexity," that reducing the number of equivalence classes reduces complexity. Siblings (multiple implementations of the same type) are the most obvious examples of equivalence classes that need elimination, but even cousin relationships offer opportunities for at least partial consolidation.

Containment relationships are key to identifying opportunities to further partition the partitions. As we partition the partitions, we dramatically reduce set complexity. Containment relationships are clear indicators that opportunities exist for lower level partitioning.

Partnership relationships are key to analyzing ABC permeability. What is ABC permeability? Recall from Chapter 3 that the definition of a partition requires that every element of a universe live in one and only one of the subsets that make up the partition and that there be no interaction between elements of different subsets. In the real world of the enterprise, this requirement can rarely be met 100 percent. For example, in the sales/inventory interaction shown earlier in Figure 4-9, there is some interaction between the two subsets. This interaction can range from highly intertwined and convoluted to highly controlled and defined.

The more intertwined the two systems are, the less they resemble an actual partition. As the separation points between subsets becomes less well-defined, it becomes more and more likely that changes to one system will have an impact on other systems.

This is what I mean by permeability. Permeability is a measure of how intertwined the two ABCs are. As ABCs become more permeable, they begin to look less like a mathematical partition and more like a pile of spaghetti in which relationships are complex, highly entangled, and impossible to sort through. We can't apply the SIP principles of complexity control to those systems because SIP is grounded in partition theory, and the more permeable the systems are, the more difficult it is to define partition boundaries.

Partner relationships show you the "thin spots" that separate ABCs. In the sales/inventory system shown back in Figure 4-8, we know there is a thin spot between sales and inventory. How thin? We can't tell from the diagram. But at least the partner relationship shows us where to look.

In most cases, ABCs interact through their technical components, as shown earlier in Figure 4-9. Therefore, it becomes especially critical to analyze the technical connections between ABC partners. Often such an analysis reveals highly convoluted technical relationships, a major problem when it comes to complexity control. In Chapter 7, "Guarding the Boundaries: Software Fortresses," I will discuss some of the approaches one can use to manage the permeability of these technical connection points.

So you can see that all the ABC relationships relate back to basic SIP principles. Implementation/deployment relationships point to partitioning failures. Type relationships point the way to equivalence class consolidation. Composition relationships point the way to additional partitioning and set reduction. And partner relationships show us where the boundaries between ABCs need to be carefully examined for violation of partitioning principles.

Retail Operation, Again

Given the richness of ABC relationships, the pre-ABC diagram of the retail operation shown in Figure 4-1 looks pretty naive in retrospect. Let's look at this operation using ABC notation. Then we can return to our original question: is this a good enterprise architecture?

Referring back to Figure 4-4, you can see the Contoso stores divided into two regions, with each region supported by a distribution center and each distribution center making purchases from multiple suppliers. So far, it sounds fine. But if you look more closely at Figure 4-4 you will notice that sometimes this pattern is altered. Here are some variants from the standard pattern:

- Store 01 also makes direct purchases from Supplier 1, bypassing the regional distribution center.

- Store 03, which straddles the two regions, sometimes makes purchases from one regional distribution center and sometimes from the other.

After discussing the retail operation with the client, the type diagram shown in Figure 4-10 emerges.

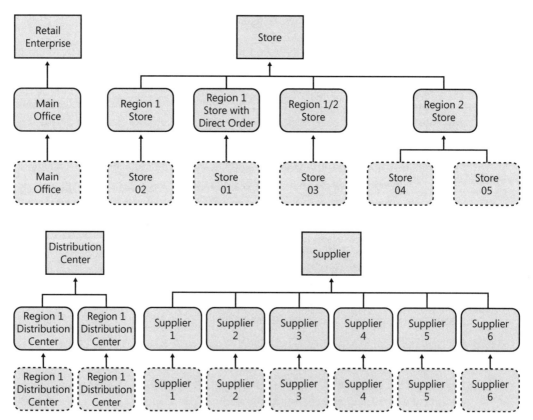

FIGURE 4-10 Type relationship diagram of Contoso retail operation.

In comparing Figures 4-4 and 4-10, we can't help but notice that the reasonable-looking Figure 4-4 has suddenly deteriorated into an ugly type relationship diagram. What does this mean? Does this mean that showing type relationships is a bad idea? No. What it means is that type relationships are better at drawing out unnecessary complexity than are the pre-ABC enterprise architectural diagrams such as Figure 4-1. The problem is not in the use of type hierarchies. The problem is in the complexity of the underlying systems. It is hard to hide complexity under the rug of type relationships.

But knowing that complexity exists is one thing. We probably didn't need SIP to tell us this system is complex. The important question is, what can we do about it?

The answer to this question is always the same. Create partitions. Strengthen the partitions. Reduce the size of the partitions. Iterate through the resulting subsets.

So let's look for ABC implementations that are unnecessary. What does an unnecessary ABC look like? It looks like a sibling. The first thought you should have when recognizing a sibling is, "Great! An opportunity for consolidation." We see three sets of siblings: stores, regional distribution centers, and suppliers. The fact that we have four sibling stores makes them a tempting target. Two sibling regional distribution centers also makes them good candidates.

The six sibling suppliers are a little different. These ABCs are not under our control. These are implemented and deployed by the companies from whom we purchase inventory. But even though they are not under our control, they are still causing us problems. The reason they cause us problems is that they all have their own unique business processes and software systems with which we must interact. This means that our regional distribution centers each maintain different connection approaches for each supplier. What can we do about this? How do we consolidate operations that are not under our control?

This might be a time when *might* can make *right*. We can try to convince the suppliers to present to the outside world (meaning, us) a single approach to ordering. If our organization has the purchasing clout to insist on this, all the better. If not, perhaps we can work within an industry consortium, because other retail operations are going to have the same problems as we will. What should our outside partners come up with? Almost anything will be an improvement, as long as they agree. It is less important what the exact types are than that the types agree.

Note that we don't really care if the suppliers have identical *implementations* of the purchasing business processes and software systems. They just need to be identical from the perspective of the outside world. Today, the most likely approach to accomplishing this is to agree on a single service-oriented interface for purchasing. This interface effectively defines the type. But the use of service-oriented interfaces is about IT technology as it exists today. Tomorrow, this might change. What will not change is that we need an agreed-upon implementation of purchasing (at least, from the perspective of the outside world) using whatever the technology *du jour* is.

Having identified Contoso's convoluted type hierarchy, we can begin to envision the changes we would like to make. Figure 4-11 shows a SIP-friendly type hierarchy for this retail operation.

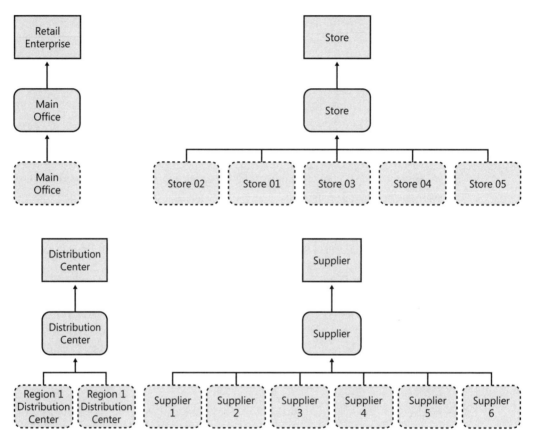

FIGURE 4-11 SIP-friendly retail hierarchy.

Now compare Figures 4-10 and 4-11. Which one do you think looks less complex? You don't have to be an expert in equivalence classes, set theory, or SIP to realize that Figure 4-11 is a much better architecture than Figure 4-10. You don't even need to know much about retailing.

It's also instructive to compare the partner relationships of the retail operation. Let's return again to the original operation, as shown in Figure 1, Based on the analysis of the type relationships, shown in Figure 4-10, we can guess quite a bit about the original partner relationships. It would have had to look something like Figure 4-12.

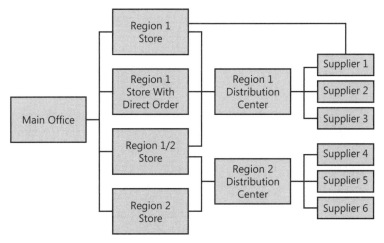

FIGURE 4-12 Partner relationships of pre-SIP retail operation.

When looking at Figure 4-12, keep in mind that every connection point represents two major problems *vis à vis* complexity. First, it represents a thin spot in the partition, a place where the partitioning is likely to be very weak. Second, it represents an interaction between two ABCs. These interactions introduce their own significant measure of complexity.

What do the partner relationships look like post-SIP analysis? Assuming that we have implemented the changes called for in the type relationship analysis, the partner relationships will look something like Figure 4-13.

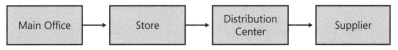

FIGURE 4-13 Partner relationships in post-SIP retail operation.

So once again, I ask the question: Which would you prefer to have as your enterprise architecture: The pre-SIP retail operation (Figure 4-12) or the post-SIP retail operation (Figure 4-13)?

And SIP still has more to offer in terms of simplification. For example, we can compare the ABC *distribution center* with similar operations across the industry. In our inventory of ABCs, we find that "industry standard" distribution center ABCs are typically composed of five lower level ABCs (for example, *define logistics strategy, operate warehouse, operate outbound transportation*) and that each of these, on average, is composed of five even lower-level ABCs.

This means that we can potentially split this equivalence class into five new equivalence classes, and we can split each of those by five others. The net result? A 94-percent reduction in the size of the equivalence classes.

Who cares? We do! Remember, huge simplification gains are made from partitioning equivalence classes into smaller partitions. It seems that we have a long way to go before we find the optimal partitioning scheme and, thus, the simplest possible architecture for our retail operation.

Summary

In this chapter, I showed how the principles of partitions, set theory, and equivalence classes all relate to enterprise architectures. I discussed these in relationship to the fundamental unit of a SIP enterprise architecture: the ABC. ABC stands for *autonomous business capability*. An ABC is composed of both business processes and software systems.

In the world of ABCs, we distinguish between types, implementations, and deployments. Types are categories of ABCs. Implementations are collections of software systems and business processes that have been designed to do something. Deployments are copies of those implementations that are put in place in a particular location to actually produce some effect.

The types of ABCs and the relationships between those types give us considerable information about the enterprise architecture, especially as it relates to complexity. ABC types help us find opportunities for ABC consolidation. ABC composition leads us to repartitioning, with the eventual aim of creating smaller equivalence classes. ABC partner relationships help us analyze the partition for soundness.

Now that we know about ABCs, the fundamental unit of the enterprise architecture, we are ready to look at process. How do we find these ABCs? That is the topic of the next chapter.

Chapter 5
SIP Process

So far, I have discussed the mathematical principles of complexity control, the role of partitions in controlling complexity, and how partitions of an enterprise architecture can be realized in *autonomous business capabilities* (ABCs). For these ABCs to result in the dramatic predicted reductions of complexity, there must be a process for their identification, description, and delivery that is well aligned with the mathematical model. This is the purpose of the SIP process.

SIP, of course, stands for *simple iterative partitions*, which is the methodology I use for controlling the complexity of enterprise architectures. Simple iterative partitions describes, at a high level, the main approaches used for complexity control: partitioning, simplification, and iterative delivery. Now let's look at this process more closely.

Overview

The overall goals of the SIP process are the same as for any enterprise architectural methodology: to align the information technology (IT) systems and business processes so that the two are working together effectively to reach the goals of the enterprise. SIP differs from other methodologies in that it is based on the premise that no alignment is possible without first controlling the complexity of the enterprise, and that once complexity has been controlled, alignment is straightforward. So, in addition to the general goals of all enterprise architectural methodologies, SIP has these unique goals:

- **Complexity Control**   No surprise here. Reducing complexity is the focal point.

- **Logic-Based Decisions**   Most enterprise architecture decisions are based on instinct, gut feeling, politics, vendor loyalty, and so on. SIP seeks to remove these emotion-based (irrational) decisions and instead approach every decision from a rational and mathematically grounded perspective.

- **Value-Driven Deliverables**   SIP is value-driven. All deliverables are measured against quantifiable business value.

- **Reproducible Results**   SIP provides a methodology that is reproducible. Two SIP practitioners analyzing a similar enterprise should come up with architectural solutions that are similar.

- **Verifiable Architectures**   SIP produces architectures that can be mathematically verified.

■ **Flexible Methodology**   SIP can be used with most other enterprise architecture methodologies because SIP completes them by addressing concerns that the other methodologies do not address and does not seek to address problems that are already well solved by other methodologies.

The SIP process, at a high level, is shown in Figure 5-1.

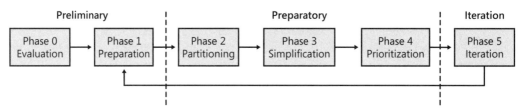

FIGURE 5-1 SIP process (overview).

As shown in Figure 5-1, the SIP process consists of six primary phases that can be roughly divided into three categories. The categories are as follows:

■ **Preliminary**   Includes all activities that typically occur as an organization is evaluating its readiness to leverage an enterprise architecture, in general, and whether SIP, specifically, is a good match for its needs. I also include the activities that introduce SIP to the enterprise.

■ **Preparatory**   Includes activities that culminate in the identification and prioritization of the enterprise partitions, guided by the mathematical models for complexity and partitioning.

■ **Iterative**   Includes the ongoing activities of designing, implementing, and delivering value-rich ABCs. If an enterprise architect is using complementary methodologies— such as Zachman, TOGAF, or FEA—this is where they fit in.

Phase 0: Enterprise Architecture Evaluation

The starting point for a SIP (or any enterprise architecture) engagement is typically an internal investigation into the potential value of creating an enterprise architecture. Although SIP can greatly reduce the cost of generating an enterprise architecture, there is no denying that creating an enterprise architecture requires time, energy, and investment from multiple individuals and groups within the organization.

Why bother? For the simple reason that the results of a well-constructed enterprise architecture can be truly transformational for an organization. However, there is no point in undertaking a SIP engagement unless you can be reasonably sure of two things. First, a successful enterprise architecture will deliver value to the enterprise. And second, that the enterprise can have a reasonable expectation of success in creating an enterprise architecture. These are the issues on which an organization should focus in Phase 0.

I began the discussion in Chapter 1, "Enterprise Architecture Today," by describing typical issues that drive many organizations to consider building an enterprise architecture. Now I will reconsider those issues, looking specifically at how a SIP approach addresses each of them.

Issue: Unreliable Enterprise Information

I discussed the need for reliable enterprise information and said that an enterprise architecture can help pinpoint data problems. This is true in theory, but in practice, most methodologies do not offer any theory as to what causes data problems or how those problems might be eliminated. SIP does.

SIP approaches data reliability as part of the overall partitioning problem. Just as functionality is to be partitioned, the data that is associated with that function is also to be partitioned. And just as SIP can help us analyze business functions for poor partitioning, so too can it help us analyze data. SIP also provides a model for how data should, and should not, be shared.

Unreliable information is frequently a result of uncoordinated data duplication across multiple IT systems that span multiple uncoordinated business processes. This is an example of high permeability at the junction points between business systems. A SIP-generated enterprise architecture minimizes the permeability at these junction points, because such permeability is considered to be incompatible with strong partitions. This is a standard part of the inspection of partner relationships, a topic I discussed in the previous chapter. SIP, therefore, can greatly increase the reliability of enterprise information.

For example, one client of mine had two legacy (pre-SIP) processes—say, A and B. Process A handed over some data to process B, which then proceeded to update that data. However, the data, as seen by process B was now different than the same data as seen by process A. A SIP analysis of this system showed that the duplication of data was adding unnecessary complexity. Once we partitioned the data according to SIP rules, we could eliminate the redundant data copy in process B and, instead, have process B request the necessary information from process A on an as-needed basis. This critical data was now consistent regardless of whether you were getting it from process A or B.

Issue: Untimely Enterprise Information

I discussed the need for not only reliable information being available to the enterprise, but reliable information being made available in a timely fashion.

Untimely information is frequently a result of highly human-driven operations. Human-driven operations are a sign that IT is not well aligned with the business needs. Although most methodologies seek this alignment, only SIP does it within the context of minimizing complexity.

A SIP enterprise architecture restructures/subdivides the business into autonomous units, and it ensures that within and across units IT is being used to its maximum capability. This, in turn, ensures that business decisions can always be based on absolutely up-to-date information. By ensuring that IT systems are used effectively to support human information handling, SIP can greatly improve the timeliness of an enterprise's information.

For example, a client of mine was trying to address a problem of untimely data in a legacy system. Data was received in various formats. While some data was visible in reports soon after receipt, other data might not be visible for weeks after receipt. A SIP analysis helped us pinpoint the partner relationships. We looked at each one carefully. One of these relationships involved the printing out of information from one process, the delivery of those printouts to a data entry clerk, and the re-entry of that information into another process. After the SIP analysis, we could redesign that particular partner relationship so that the information transfer operation between the two processes was handled automatically and much more efficiently.

Issue: New Complex Projects Underway

I discussed how the initiation of a new complex project frequently triggers curiosity about enterprise architecture. At this point, it should go without saying that SIP is highly focused on controlling the complexity of IT projects, greatly improving the odds of a project's success. The simpler the project, the greater the odds of success. By transforming complex projects into simple projects, SIP substantially improves the odds of success.

For example, a client of mine was preparing to undertake a very large rewrite of a failing legacy system. The complexity of the project was overwhelming. Nobody could see where to start. A SIP analysis allowed us to break up the project into a manageable number of much smaller, much simpler projects that could be delivered in an iterative approach.

Issue: New Companies Being Acquired

I discussed how enterprises acquiring new companies frequently try to use enterprise architecture to help understand how the business processes and IT systems of the two organizations might match up. SIP helps an organization understand the lines of autonomy between functions. Understanding which functions are autonomous from which other functions makes it much easier to merge the two systems together. If either, or both, companies do not have a SIP-like enterprise architecture, creating one will probably be the best first step to a successful merger. SIP's ABCs are excellent candidates for packaging functionality together and for helping the parties involved acquire an understanding of how the functions of one organization relate to the functions of the other.

For example, in Chapter 4, "The ABCs of Enterprise Partitions," I described a semi-fictional client named Contoso (not a real name). Contoso is a retailing operation. If the company wanted to acquire another retail company, it would be much easier to do so if it understood how the new client's retail systems (both business processes and IT systems) could be assimilated into Contoso's existing systems. A SIP analysis could be used to identify the autonomous units of the two organizations and how they might best work together (or alternatively, what problems Contoso might face when it tries to assimilate the other organization's systems).

Issue: Enterprise Wants to Spin Off Unit

I discussed how corporate spin-offs drive enterprise architectures, because an architectural analysis will show which functions are autonomous. Other methodologies do not have a formal definition for what is meant by *autonomous,* nor a test to see if a given function is or is not autonomous with respect to the rest of the enterprise. SIP includes both a formal definition of and a test for autonomy. These autonomous functions are the easiest to spin-off.

We can look once again to Contoso to see how this might work. Recall from Chapter 4 that Contoso had both retail operations and regional distribution centers. Suppose Contoso decided to get out of the retail business and focus only on wholesale operations. In this case, it would want to spin off the retail stores. This process would be facilitated by a clear understanding of how the retail operations interoperate with the wholesale operations. A SIP analysis would look at both retail and wholesale operations as autonomous operations (ABCs) that were connected together by a small number of well-defined partnership relationships.

Issue: Need to Identify Outsourcing Opportunities

I discussed how the need to outsource can drive enterprise architectures. This is another area in which the SIP focus on autonomy can really pay off. The more autonomous a given function is, the less intertwined it is with other business functions and the easier that function will be to outsource. This analysis is very difficult to perform unless the enterprise has an architecture that focuses on well-defined, autonomous units. SIP is an ideal methodology for such an architecture, and the SIP-generated ABCs are well positioned for outsourcing.

Again, Contoso provides a good example. Contoso is a hypothetical retail operation. Human resources is not an operation that is likely to differentiate Contoso in its business area, and therefore Contoso might well decide that this could be outsourced. However, to outsource such an operation, Contoso must be able to understand the relationships between its human resources operations and the rest of its processes. The best way to do this is to use SIP to generate an ABC map of the enterprise.

Issue: Regulatory Requirements

I discussed the difficulty of complying with regulatory requirements, with their insistence on understanding why, how, and under what circumstances data is updated. Although any enterprise architecture should try to explain the relationship between data updates and business functionality, in reality this is almost impossible to accomplish unless the data is partitioned alongside the business functionality and IT solutions. Without a formal notion of partitioning, this objective will be almost impossible to achieve. SIP's ABCs provide such a formal notion of partitioning. A SIP-generated enterprise architecture that focuses on simplification and autonomy of systems will go a long way toward helping enterprises meet increasingly common regulatory requirements.

As an example, one of my clients is in the health care field. This field is highly regulated and many of the regulations deal with the confidentiality of patient data. Considerable effort was put into their legacy system to ensure patient confidentiality, but the client was not sure that it would survive an audit. A SIP analysis allowed us to quickly get an overview of ABC partner relationships. Each of these relationships represents an entryway into the system, By focusing only on the partner relationships, we could quickly identify two areas where client data could be compromised. Once we knew where the potential leaks were, we were able to design appropriate security measures.

Issue: Need to Automate Relationships with External Partners

I discussed the trend in the business world to automate relationships between partners. Any methodology should ensure that the technology is well aligned with the business functions, and this technology should be available for automation. Unfortunately, most methodologies do not have a formal model for how autonomous units (such as those we would expect to find between partners) should work together. These systems need well-defined entry points that allow systems to interoperate with an absolute minimum of dependencies. This concept of minimal dependency closely maps to the SIP notion of minimum partition permeability. The SIP model for ABCs includes a definition for partner relationships, and it defines the common communications patterns that are ideally suited for automating external relation-ships. This and the strong SIP focus on autonomy allows ABCs to work highly effectively with today's technologies, such as Simple Object Access Protocol (SOAP) and other Web service interoperability standards.

As an example, one of my clients is in the public sector and it needs to interoperate with federal authorities. A SIP analysis helped us define the necessary partner relationships that would allow the interoperability while minimizing the disruption to the existing systems.

Issue: Need to Automate Relationships with Customers

I discussed the value of an enterprise architecture in helping automate customer interactions. This automation places demands on both the IT systems and the business processes. Many of the requirements of automated partner relationships (the previous issue in this list) also apply here, although the customer relationships will be mediated by browser-facing systems rather than service-facing systems. Still, simplicity, autonomy, and well-defined entry points are critical to success in this area. These goals are difficult to realize in a cost-effective manner without a SIP-like enterprise architecture.

As an example, one of my clients operates a call center to allow its customers to check on the status of work requests they have placed. Our SIP analysis shows how the new client-facing browser system will interact with the client's existing IT systems.

Issue: Poor Relationship Between IT and Business Units

I discussed the common problem of poor relationships between business and IT groups. Any enterprise architectural methodology should seek to bring these two groups together. The reality is, however, that all too often the business groups see enterprise architecture as yet another expensive project championed by IT that is unlikely to deliver any value. Understandably, the business units have little interest in taking part in this exercise, and without their support, no enterprise architectural effort can hope to succeed.

SIP is different. My experience with multiple clients is that the ABCs offer common ground for both IT and the business groups. The business units quickly get involved in the effort because they see quick results in the delivery of ABCs to which they can relate. They also intuitively understand the problem of complexity and the business value of getting complexity under control.

SIP teaches that business is not the enemy. IT is not the enemy. Complexity is the enemy.

Issue: Poor Interoperability of IT Systems

I discussed the problems caused when IT systems are unable to interoperate. All methodologies argue in favor of interoperability, but only SIP offers a specific approach for achieving interoperability. Interoperability is best achieved through the use of well-documented and low-dependency juncture points. SIP, with its focus on architecture with high autonomy and low permeability between ABCs is ideal for this scenario.

Issue: IT Systems Unmanageable

I discussed the problem of unmanageable IT systems and pointed out the relationship between this and IT systems that have poor interoperability. The inability to manage IT systems is directly related to the complexity of those IT systems. Manage the complexity of the IT systems and you will be able to manage the IT systems themselves. The solution, of course, is to leverage SIP's focus on simplification through partitioning and autonomy. SIP-architected systems are able to work independently of each other, but they still have the ability to interoperate through well-defined partner relationships.

Contraindications

As you can see, a number of common problems that plague enterprises can be eliminated with a SIP-like enterprise architecture. However, being able to benefit from SIP is not a sufficient reason to undertake a SIP engagement. One must also be reasonably confident in the eventual success of that undertaking. To be fair, then, I will discuss what factors might be contraindications (that is, factors arguing *against* using SIP).

In my experience, there are two scenarios in which SIP's (or any enterprise architecture methodology's) chances for success are reduced. The first is when the enterprise architecture initiative is not supported at the highest management levels of the enterprise. SIP, or any enterprise architecture methodology, can be successful only when it enjoys the support of senior management. Enterprise architectures drive not just changes in IT systems, but changes in business processes and, perhaps even more importantly, changes in patterns of human relationships.

These changes cannot be driven either by the business group or by the IT group. It must be driven at a high enough level so that both groups are highly incentivized to make the effort work. This kind of cooperation is often without precedent in an organization, and it usually requires a clear mandate from a level at or very close to the CEO.

The other contraindication I have seen is organizations in which the relationship between the business and IT groups has gone beyond the normal bickering and finger-pointing and has degenerated into a highly pathological pattern of distrust and animosity. Such organizations require intervention therapy that goes well beyond the training of an enterprise architect.

So is your organization a candidate for an enterprise architecture in general and a SIP methodology in particular? I think it is if you can answer yes to the following three questions:

- Does your organization have one or more problems similar to those mentioned here?

- Is your organization committed at the highest levels of management to solving these problems?

- Is there a reasonably healthy (or at least not pathologically unhealthy) relationship between the IT and business groups?

Did you answer *yes* to all three questions? If so, you are ready for an enterprise architecture-driven solution. And if you see complexity as an important issue, you will find the SIP approach particularly attractive. Whatever you decide, this decision is your main goal to reach in Phase 0.

Phase 1: SIP Preparation

If you have made it to Phase 1, you have completed your self-assessment, decided that you are a good candidate for an enterprise architecture, and have chosen SIP (or something like SIP) as your methodology of choice. Congratulations!

Phase 1 is where we set the stage for a successful SIP engagement. The first thing you will want to do is acquire some SIP expertise, either in the form of internal training or in the form of external consulting. Although it is tempting to save a few bucks by minimizing the use of outside expertise, I recommend against it. I know, as a consultant myself, I have my own bias. But many millions of dollars, and sometimes far more, can be saved by getting the right expertise in-house at the beginning of a project.

After all, you are getting ready to lay the foundations for your future IT investments. The success or failure of these early efforts could well decide the future viability of your enterprise. It is essential that this effort be solid.

There are typically five main deliverables from Phase 1:

- An audit of organizational readiness
- Training that introduces the need for controlling complexity and that introduces the SIP methodology
- Determination and documentation of the chosen governance model
- Determination and documentation of how SIP will blend in with other organizational processes and methodologies
- Customization of enterprise-specific tools

Let's go through these deliverables. Keep in mind that there is interplay between them. For example, in the course of training, new ideas can come up that can influence other deliverables, such as the best SIP blend for the organization.

Audit of Organizational Readiness

Our first step is to take a sanity check on your readiness for building an enterprise architecture in general, and using SIP, in particular. I know, you just did this in Phase 0, but the only thing worse than needing an enterprise architecture and not doing it, is needing it, doing it, and failing. That hurts everybody. So look closely at the level of executive commitment, the psychological health of the organization, and the nature of the problems you are trying to solve. If you have done a good job in Phase 0, you should be able to move through this part quickly.

Training

Most individuals, especially in IT, think of complexity, at worst, as a necessary evil and, at best, as job security. We want to change this attitude. To do this, we will conduct training that demonstrates the true nature of complexity. Complexity is not cute. It is evil. It is expensive and destructive. It is the foe, the adversary, the villain. It is not a problem to be managed; it is a disease to be eradicated. It is ugly. It is nasty. It stains all it touches. It is public enemy number one.

And, of course, it is unnecessary. This training typically includes enough instruction on the math of complexity and partitioning so that participants will, at least, understand the basic principles of complexity control.

Training is also conducted on the SIP methodology as it has been customized for this enterprise, or the SIP blend that I discussed earlier.

Governance Model

Before going too far down the enterprise architecture path, you will need an organizational model for how enterprise architecture decisions will be made and how responsibilities will be delegated. SIP differs from most enterprise architecture methodologies in that it minimizes the number of decisions that must be made at the enterprise level. It does this by putting as many decisions as possible in the *implementation* category and then delegating those decisions to the groups responsible for implementing them.

For example, many organizations try to create a single view of data across the enterprise and then assume that responsibility for this view will be owned by the enterprise architecture team. In my experience, this approach is incredibly time-consuming and rarely successful. I believe that a significant swatch of complexity can be removed by saying that data storage is an implementation issue. However, data must not be confused with knowledge, and the enterprise architecture team needs to be responsible for directing policies that are related to enterprisewide knowledge integrity.

Some of the other governance issues that need to be decided include the following:

- Composition of the enterprise architecture team
- Reporting structure of the enterprise architecture team
- Process for introducing new ABCs into the enterprise architecture
- Ownership and management of the SIP blend (discussed in the next section)

- Ownership and management of ABC and type inventories

- Ownership of management of technical infrastructure

- Application responsibilities for supporting the enterprise knowledge base

- Management and structure of ABC teams

- Process for documenting enterprise architecture

For some organizations, it makes sense to put off some of these decisions until the delivery of a few high-visibility ABCs. This will help generate enthusiasm for the overall SIP approach.

SIP Blend

SIP is not intended to replace other enterprise architectural methodologies, but to augment them in the specific area of complexity control. The SIP process defines ABCs as the basic building block of the enterprise, but once these ABCs have been defined, some method needs to be followed to document the business requirements of the ABC and how the technical systems will meet those needs.

The best way to think of the relationship between SIP and other methodologies is that SIP is about identifying and architecting ABCs. After these ABC definitions have been finalized and validated against the mathematical models, other methodologies can be used to architect and design the implementation of the ABC itself.

As I discussed in Chapter 1, there are several other enterprise architecture methodologies and all have ideas that can be leveraged. Zachman, for example, offers a good taxonomy for categorizing architectural artifacts. The Open Group Architectural Framework (TOGAF) includes a good process for driving an ABC implementation architecture. Federal Enterprise Architecture (FEA) has good ideas for tracking maturity levels of different organizations within the enterprise. And some customers take a quite different approach, that once the architecture has been SIP-ified, the remaining pieces are so simple that you don't need any other methodologies.

There is no right answer here. The organizational politics, formality, and demographics all play roles in choosing the best possible SIP blend. But whatever is going to be used needs to be decided, documented, and rolled out to the various groups at this time.

Enterprise-Specific Tools

A number of SIP-related tools need to be specialized for individual enterprises. One of the most important of these is the Value-Graph Analysis Tool that is used to prioritize candidate ABCs for implementation. I will discuss value graphs in the Phase 4 section, where they play their major role.

Phase 2: Partitioning

By the time we get to Phase 2, we have laid the groundwork and we are starting on creating an enterprise architecture. The overall goal of this phase is to lay out a collection of ABCs, each of which represents an equivalence class, and therefore, a subset of a partition of the enterprise. Each of these ABCs should be as fine-grained as possible within the constraints of the equivalence relation *synergistic*.

The process of partitioning an enterprise starts with the highest possible view of the enterprise and treats the enterprise as a whole as a discrete autonomous business capability (ABC) type. We then attempt to partition that ABC type. In other words, we decompose it into lower level ABC types that, taken as a group, represent a partition of the original ABC type. If we are successful, we can continue this process with each of the lower level ABCs.

So as we discover an ABC type called *retail*, for example, and decide that it is composed of the types *sales, inventory,* and *reporting,* we also want to assign the type *retail* within the overall type hierarchy we use in our enterprise. The ownership of this type library is one of the ownership issues that should have been decided in Phase 1, as part of governance.

We often don't follow every possible path of ABC decomposition. We follow only paths that are of interest to our immediate goals. We won't ignore ABCs that are not on our critical path, we will just save those for another day when we are trying to improve something in those areas.

So let's go through this, step by step. Let's say we want to completely change the way our fictitious company Contoso (introduced in Chapter 4) manages in-store inventory. We start with the highest level ABC. Figure 5-2 shows the highest level ABC decomposed into four lower level ABCs, with the path we will be following highlighted.

FIGURE 5-2 Highest level retail decomposition.

Let's follow the trail down toward in-store inventory. Adding the next level gives us something like Figure 5-3.

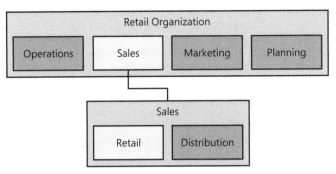

FIGURE 5-3 Another level of decomposition.

We still haven't "found" our inventory system, so we need to continue down, as shown in Figure 5-4.

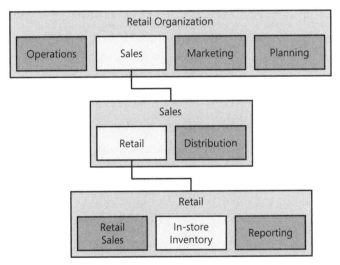

FIGURE 5-4 Final level of decomposition.

At this point, we have found the ABC of interest. We have also identified nine other ABCs that play a role in our enterprise. We also want to assign type hierarchies. As you recall from Chapter 4, type hierarchies represent relationships between ABCs, going from the most general to the most specific. One possible type hierarchy for these ABCs is shown in Figure 5-5.

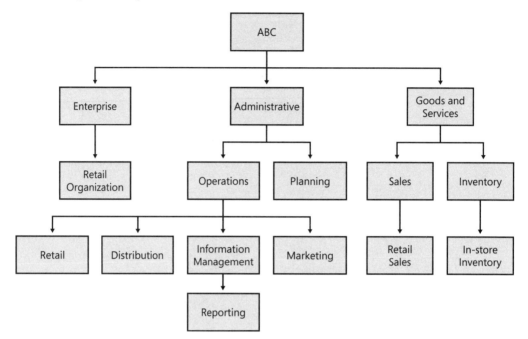

FIGURE 5-5 Type hierarchies.

We also want to describe our expected implementations and deployments. With this information, our ABC takes on more body, as shown in Figure 5-6.

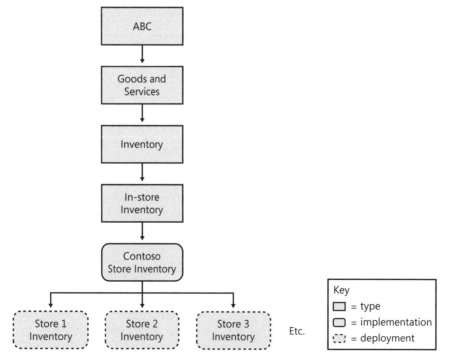

FIGURE 5-6 Detailed information on inventory.

The final concern of Phase 2 is documenting the ABC of interest (*In-store Inventory*). We are not going to get into implementation details, but we do need to know information such as the following:

- Business requirements

- User scenarios

- Success indicators

SIP does not dictate what information should be captured or how it should be captured. There are many processes used within organizations to document this information, and the exact blend of those processes will have been determined in Phase 1 (*SIP Preparation*).

Phase 3: Partition Simplification

Let's review where we are at this point. We have identified the type of the ABC type of interest to our immediate project. The ABC type is *In-store Inventory*. We have also identified the name of the specific implementation that we will eventually be delivering. This is *Contoso Store Inventory*. We have indicated that we expect to have one deployment of this ABC in each of our store locations. And finally, we have documented the business requirements of the inventory system.

We have also successively partitioned our enterprise. Figure 5-2, for example, showed the high-level enterprise (retail organization) partitioned into four subclasses. Figure 5-3 showed one of these subclasses (*Sales*) partitioned into two other subclasses. Figure 5-4 showed the *Retail* subclass further partitioned into three subclasses, one of which, *In-store Inventory*, is the particular subclass, or ABC, of interest.

We have also documented the expected implementation and deployment pattern of this ABC. Figure 5-6 shows that we will have one implementation of the In-store Inventory type, that this implementation will be called *Contoso Store Inventory*, and that this implementation will be deployed in each of the retail Contoso stores.

The question of concern in the current phase is this: have we done the best possible job of partitioning from the perspective of complexity control? In particular, is there any possible further simplification of the *Contoso Store Inventory*?

As we go through this process, we want to keep in mind the five laws of partitions that I first presented in Chapter 2, "A First Look at Complexity." Here are the five laws of partitions again:

- **First Law of Partitions**   Partitions must be true partitions. From an enterprise architectural perspective, this means that every piece of enterprise functionality must live in one and only ABC.

- **Second Law of Partitions**   Partition definitions must be appropriate. From an enterprise architectural perspective, this means that the decomposition of ABCs should yield ABCs that make sense from an organizational perspective. Executives should be able to visualize ABCs as something that maps to the enterprise.

- **Third Law of Partitions**   Partition numbers must be appropriate. From an enterprise architectural perspective, this means that each ABC should decompose into three to eight ABCs, with four a common, manageable number.

- **Fourth Law of Partitions**   Partition sizes must be roughly equal. From an enterprise architectural perspective, this means that when an ABC is decomposed, each lower level ABC should be roughly equal in terms of complexity, organizational resources, and organizational visibility.

- **Fifth Law of Partitions**   Partition interactions must be minimal and well defined. From an enterprise architectural perspective, this means that ABCs that have partner relationships (discussed in Chapter 4) should interact with each other in a minimal number of well-defined ways.

We can add to these laws several issues that came up in Chapter 3, "Mathematics of Complexity," around the topic of simplification. The first of these issues was the concept of synergy as an equivalence relation. I'll state this as the First Law of Simplification:

> *Subclasses of a partition should be constructed with the synergistic equivalence relation. From an enterprise architecture perspective, this means that an ABC should be further decomposed, if possible, so that functionality is distributed across lower level ABCs by synergy. In other words, by placing together functionality that is logically inseparable.*

We also found that in addition to subpartitioning, there was another approach to simplification: function removal. I'll state this as the Second Law of Simplification:

> *Any functionality that can be removed from an ABC should be removed.*

Let's start with the First Law of Simplification: continue partitioning. As we apply this to the Contoso Store Inventory system, we might well decide that further partitioning is possible. For example, the Contoso Store Inventory might be decomposed into Inventory Receiving, Inventory Removal, Inventory Reporting, Inventory Locations, and Inventory Replenish. We can indicate this new partitioning with an ABC diagram for Contoso Store Inventory, shown in Figure 5-7.

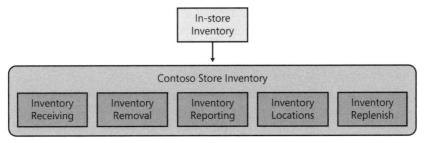

FIGURE 5-7 Contoso store inventory ABC diagram.

There are several approaches we can take to function removal (the Second Law of Simplification), and all should be explored. One thing we want to do is look closely at the business requirements. Are all of them absolutely necessary? Do people understand the cost? Do people understand how much each will add to the overall complexity of the project; to the time it will take to deliver the project? Are there any that can be relegated to future releases of the project?

Another approach to function removal is to look for consolidation opportunities. Do we already have an implementation of this type? Can we tweak that implementation rather than create a whole new implementation?

We can also look for outsourcing opportunities. If this is an ABC that is not central to our overall mission, perhaps we are better off focusing on core differentiating functionality. Outsourcing comes in various flavors, from outsourcing implementations, to purchasing prepackaged systems, to using a packaged outside service.

We also need to understand the partner relationships. Figure 5-8 shows us how these might now work with each other and noninventory ABCs.

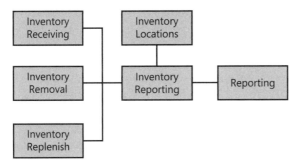

FIGURE 5-8 Partner ABC relationship.

These figures are all helpful in giving us a sense that we are making progress, but pretty pictures aren't enough. We need to look at our work against the laws of partitioning and simplification. So let's go through them.

The First Law of Partitions says that the partition of Contoso Store Inventory must be a true partition, meaning every piece of functionality originally identified for Contoso Store Inventory must live in one, and only one, of the lower level ABCs. To do this, we need to check the functional specifications for the original ABC and the decomposed set of ABCs and make sure that every functional specification is accounted for.

The Second Law of Partitions says that partition definitions must be appropriate from an organizational perspective. Most executives would look at the collection of inventory ABCs and feel comfortable with them.

The Third Law of Partitions says the decomposition of ABCs should yield a reasonable number. We have found five lower level ABCs, which is entirely reasonable.

The Fourth Law of Partitions says that the ABCs resulting from the decomposition should be roughly equal in terms of size, functionality, and visibility. These ABCs all seem reasonably close.

The Fifth Law of Partitions says that the partner ABCs must have minimal and well-defined interactions. This needs to be tested against the partner relationships. We don't have enough information from Figure 5-8 to answer these questions, but it does point out where we should be looking. We will need to revisit this issue as we flesh out implementation details, especially in the technical architectures.

Okay, we have our partitions defined. Now what?

Phase 4: ABC Prioritization

Our collection of candidate ABCs is as follows:

- Inventory Receiving
- Inventory Removal
- Inventory Replenish
- Inventory Locations
- Inventory Reporting

The next step is to decide on the order of ABC implementation. These are candidates because they are the ABCs that partition the inventory functionality. How will your organization choose which project to fund and the order in which to fund them?

If your organization is like most others, it will use one of the following processes to choose:

- Fund the project that has the most aggressive champion

- Fund the project whose champion has the highest organizational rank

- Fund the project whose champion has the best political connections

- Fund the project that has the best Microsoft PowerPoint presentation

- Fund the project that promises the highest return on investment (ROI)

The last point sounds like a useful approach to prioritizing funding, but in reality, it delivers less than it should. Most organizations claim to use ROI to determine project investment, whereas, in fact, they use some combination of the first four techniques to determine project investment. It should be obvious that the first four (commonly used) choice criteria are poor predictors of eventual business value. What might not be as obvious is that ROI (the fifth criteria listed) is not much better.

The problem with ROI is that it is so easily manipulated. Out of the hundreds of ROI-based project justifications I have seen, not one was based on reproducible measurements and methodical analysis. Mostly ROI analysis is of the nature of, "We will save hundreds of millions of dollars by reduced support costs," with little supporting evidence and no follow-up analysis.

And even though many organizations say they use an ROI model, most never take the time to actually compute ROI at the end of the project. They are usually too busy trying to correct mistakes to engage in the luxury of ROI analysis.

The more projects from which an organization must choose, the lower the odds of successfully choosing the project that will deliver the best business value for the cost. For this reason, I advocate a method for assigning priorities that is based on logic and sound decision-making and, as much as possible, immune from political influence.

You can decide on any number of approaches to prioritizing projects. Whatever you do choose, this process should be one of the deliverables of Phase 1. The approach that I prefer is one I call Value Graph Analysis.

Value Graph Analysis takes into account not only the potential payoff of a project, but also the risk and a number of other factors. The theory is that if two projects have similar costs and returns, the one with the least risk should be undertaken. And if all other factors are roughly equivalent, the one with the quickest time to value should be undertaken.

A given value graph is almost as unique to a project as a fingerprint is to an individual (not quite, but close!). The specific factors for Value Graph Analysis might be tailored to an organization, but for most purposes, our defaults will work fine. The eight default factors we include in our typical Value Graph Analysis are these:

- **Market Drivers**   What market forces favor this project?

- **Cost**   What is the cost of doing this project?

- **Organizational Risk**   What are the nontechnical risk factors?

- **Technical Risk**   What are the technical risk factors?

- **Financial Value**   What is the financial value?

- **Organizational Preparedness**   How ready is the organization to undertake this project?

- **Team Readiness**   How ready is the team to undertake this project?

- **Status Quo**   What is the outcome of not doing this project?

Each of these factors has a number of inputs that are aggregated to form a composite measurement factor. For example, the factor *market driver* includes input on all of the following:

- How much the project will reduce the cost of doing business.

- How much the project will increase revenue.

- How much the project will improve competitive positioning.

- How much the project will improve service levels.

- How much the project will help roll out new products.

- How much the project will improve internal processes.

- How much the project will improve customer relationships.

Not all of these considerations need be given equal weight. For example, some organizations are focused more on the cost of doing business than they are on improving customer relationships. Those organizations can weight the consideration of cost higher than the consideration of customer relationships.

Not all of these factors will be appropriate to consider for all organizations. For example, public sector organizations often do not have revenue, so they might choose to ignore that factor or replace it with one that is more relevant.

A typical value graph is shown in Figure 5-9.

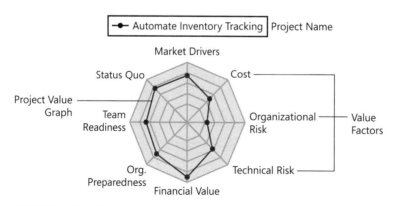

FIGURE 5-9 Typical value graph.

As you can see in Figure 5-9, each of the value factors becomes an axis on the value graph. Values that are closer to the center of the value graph are considered negative. Values closer to the edge are considered positive.

The advantage of Value Graph Analysis is that the priority of different projects can be objectively compared and assigned on the basis of their visually descriptive value graphs. For example, Figure 5-10 shows two value graphs for two candidate ABCs. Visually, it is fairly obvious that the ABC on the left is a lower priority than the one on the right.

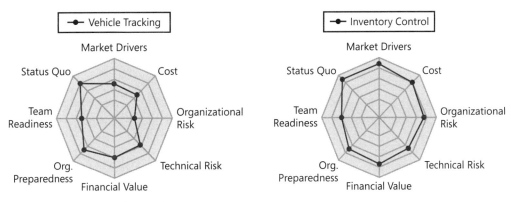

FIGURE 5-10 Two ABC value graphs.

We are making great progress. We have mapped out our enterprise as an ABC map. We have identified the ABCs that must be implemented and prioritized them. The only thing left is to deliver.

Phase 5: ABC Iteration

Delivery occurs in Phase 5, the final and most important phase. Here, iteration begins. The process iterates through the ABCs that were first identified in Phase 2, it is simplified in Phase 3, and finally it is prioritized in Phase 4. In Phase 5, the goods are delivered.

Surprisingly, this phase is the one in which SIP is most flexible and on which SIP has the least opinions. The reason for this is that most organizations already have in place good procedures for documenting business requirements, architecting IT systems, and delivering software.

There are multiple methodologies that work well in this phase, including TOGAF, ZIFA's Zachman framework, Microsoft's Solution Framework, and IBM's Unified Process. We don't believe that SIP should reinvent the wheel or dictate the process in areas that are not relevant to the problem SIP set out to solve (and hopefully, by now you know what that is—reducing complexity!).

By the time we hit Phase 5, SIP's work is largely done. It has transformed a world that once seemed hopelessly complex into a world made up of manageable, autonomous, value-rich, bite-sized morsels. Implement and deliver these morsels anyway you choose.

Of course, I am not totally opinion-less on the topic of good implementation strategies. But my opinions are more in the nature of a checklist. Do you have a process for documenting business requirements? For managing architectural artifacts? For establishing program requirements? For measuring milestones? For showing delivered value? What do we think is the best way to do these things? Most likely, the best way to do these things is the way you have already been doing them.

Summary

SIP stands for *simple iterative partitions*. The SIP process is a six-phase process, the first of which is typically done internally and often in an ad hoc way. The other five phases are the following:

- Preparation, in which the ground work for a successful SIP engagement is laid.

- Partitioning, in which the enterprise, in general, and the project, in particular, is laid out as a collection of ABCs, each of which has a type, compositional hierarchy, and deployment pattern.

- Partition Simplification, in which the collection of project ABCs is simplified as much as humanly possible.

- Prioritization, in which the collection is assigned an implementation order based on logic and analysis.

- Implementation, in which ABCs are implemented and delivered.

In the next chapter, I will look at a real-life case study of a highly complex enterprise and consider how SIP could have been used to greatly improve the odds of project success.

Chapter 6
A Case Study in Complexity

Let's take a look at a real-life case study of a complex system. There are three important lessons to be learned here. The first is how complexity creeps into a project, even one with the benefit of extensive planning. The second is how this unchecked complexity leads to project failure, even one with seemingly unlimited resources. The third is how Simple Iterative Partitions (SIP) might have saved this project, even when it was well into failure mode.

The case study I'll discuss is one of the largest and most complex systems yet tackled by any government organization. It is the National Program for Information Technology (NPfIT), a program run by the British Government's National Health Service (NHS). Sometimes NPfIT is referred to simply as the National Program, or, as they say in Britain, the National Programme. Remember these acronyms—NPfIT and NHS—you will be seeing a lot of them in this chapter.

Overview of NPfIT

NPfIT was launched in June 2002. The basic goal of NPfIT was, and continues to be, to automate and centralize the massive recordkeeping that is the backbone of its national health care system run by the NHS. Health care in Britain is mostly nationalized, unlike the United States where health care is mostly ad hoc. This centralized system creates a unique opportunity to standardize the recordkeeping of a very large number of patients and health care providers. NPfIT is promising the following capabilities when completed:

- Automation of all patient care information.

- Access to any patient record by any authorized health care professional in the UK

- Ability for primary health care staff to book appointments for patients with any other health care worker in any health care facility in the UK

- Automation of prescription services

The NHS describes NPfIT systems as follows:

> *A key aim of the National Program [NPfIT] is to give healthcare professionals access to patient information safely, securely and easily, whenever and wherever it is needed. The National Program is an essential element in delivering The NHS Plan. It is creating a multi-billion pound infrastructure which will improve patient*

care by enabling clinicians and other NHS staff to increase their efficiency and effectiveness.[1]

In a nutshell, the NPfIT promises an integrated system connecting every patient, physician, laboratory, pharmacy, and health care facility in the UK. NPfIT functionality can be loosely divided into three main categories: regional clinical information systems (CIS), infrastructure systems, and shared applications. The NPfIT architecture is shown in Figure 6-1.

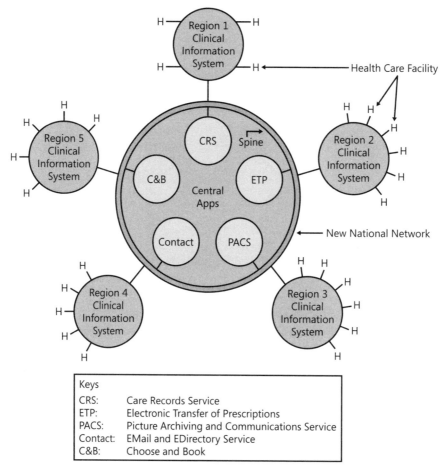

FIGURE 6-1 NPfIT architecture.

Regional clinical information systems connect health care providers (for example, hospitals, clinics, and physician offices) within a geographic area and provide their main point of contact for NPfIT. These are shown as the "hairy spheres" hanging off the central sphere shown in Figure 6-1.

---

[1] "The National Program for IT Implementation Guide," December 2006.

By my estimates, the regional clinical information systems account for approximately 79 percent of the total initial budget for NPfIT, approximately $9.8 billion. Keep in mind that NPfIT expenses are given in British pounds, and I have converted these numbers to U.S. dollars. These costing numbers are based on conflicting source data and a fluctuating exchange rate, so take these estimates as educated guesses.

Infrastructure systems will provide connectivity, security, and directory services to the NPfIT. These infrastructure systems include the New National Network (N3), which provides the network facilities, and the spine, which includes shared software facilities such as directory services. Care Records Service (CRS), the shared patient records, is sometimes shown as part of the spine and sometimes as separate shared applications.

After the regional clinical information systems, the infrastructure is the second largest part of the NPfIT budget, accounting for approximately 18 percent of the initial NPfIT budget, or $2.3 billion.

Shared coordinated activity across the entire NPfIT system appears to make up a relatively small part of the overall NPfIT budget, less than 5 percent, or about $300 million. The most important of these shared applications include the following:

- **Choose and Book**   A system that allows an appointment to be booked for any patient at any facility in the system

- **Electronic Transfer of Prescriptions**   A system that allows prescriptions to be entered for any patient in the system and filled by any pharmacy in the system

- **Picture Archiving and Communications Service**   A system that allows the central storage and retrieval of picture data, especially x-rays

The amount of data that must be coordinated is immense. According to the NHS[2], in a typical week the NHS processes

- Six million patient visits to general practitioners

- Over 64,500 emergency calls by NHS ambulances

- 360,000 patient x-rays

- 13.7 million NHS prescriptions

The NHS estimates that NPfIt will need to coordinate about 3 million critical processes and 30 million transactions per day.

The NPfIT geography is split into five *clusters*, or regional groups of patients and health care providers. The NPfIT budget is almost $2 billion per cluster. The clusters are arranged as follows:

- North East (which includes Tees Valley, Northumberland, South Yorkshire, West Yorkshire)

---

2 "The National Program for IT Implementation Guide," December 2006.

- North West and West Midland (which includes Greater Manchester, Cheshire)

- Eastern (which includes Essex, Trent)

- London

- Southern (which includes Avon, Dorset, Thames Valley)

The initial budget was allocated in 2004 among many different vendors. The highly lucrative regional cluster contracts each had a primary vendor, a CIS vendor, and other miscellaneous secondary vendors. The primary and CIS vendors awarded to each region is shown in Figure 6-2.

	Regional Cluster				
	North East	North West and West Midland	Eastern	London	Southern
Primary Vendor	Accenture	CSC	Accenture	BT	Fujitsu
CIS Vendor	iSoft	iSoft	iSoft	IDX	IDX

FIGURE 6-2 Primary and CIS vendors by regional cluster.

So NPfIT is a multibillion-dollar project split between at least a dozen vendors spread over a geographic territory of close to 100,000 square miles; it offers services to 60 million people and is expected to process over 300 transactions per second. I would call this project highly complex.

Now that you have a basic overview of NPfIT, let's see how well this project did using traditional architectural approaches. Perhaps you will recognize ghosts of your own projects in this description.

Current Status of NPfIT

NPfIT has been in crisis almost from the first day. By mid-2004 (barely a year into the contract), both Fujitsu and BT, two of the five primary regional vendors, were having trouble with their IDX (regional CIS vendor) relationships, and this trouble never let up. According to a confidential draft audit by the National Audit Office (NAO, a British government audit office),

> By mid-2004 NHS Connecting for Health was concerned about the effectiveness of supplier management of both BT and Fujitsu, and the performance of IDX... However, by April 2005, even though NHS Connecting for Health [the British government bureau responsible for NPfIT] had been applying increasing pressure, working with the prime contractors, to encourage IDX to match its planned deliveries, insufficient progress had been demonstrated and Fujitsu lost confidence in IDX's ability to deliver the Common Solution project.

The CSC/iSOFT partnership was faring little better. According to that same confidential NAO audit,

> CSC, the Local Service Provider for the North West Cluster, agreed to a remediation plan with NHS Connecting for Health for the delivery of Phase 1 Release 1 as it was having problems meeting the original target dates... Further delays led to a second remediation plan which pushed the deployment dates for two elements of Phase 1 Release 1 further back into 2006, some 19 to 22 months later than originally planned.

But of all the partnerships, the one that probably fared the worst was the Accenture/iSOFT partnership. By September 2006, Accenture had decided that the pain associated with this project was not worth it, and abandoned the project altogether. According to a baseline case study[3] in so doing it walked away from almost $4 billion in revenue writing off $500 million it had already spent, and agreeing to pay $100 million "to settle its legal obligations."

iSOFT was involved in three of the four partnerships, and the strain on that company might bankrupt it or, at the very least, force its sale. According to its financial results released in December 2006, the company took an almost $800-million loss for the fiscal year ending in April 2006—a huge loss for a company that had total revenues of the year of only $340 million.[4]

As you can see, every major company involved in the regional clusters has taken a severe financial hit from NPfIT. It seemed that everybody underestimated the complexity of this project. The costs of this underestimation will likely be measured in the tens of billions of dollars.

In the area of user confidence, NPfIT is in serious trouble. There are three critical constituencies that have been alienated by NHS's approach to NPfIT: health care workers, patients, and IT professionals.

A good indication of how the health care professionals feel about NPfIT is found in a recent editorial of the British Journal of General Practice (May 2005). It says,

> The impact on patients and professionals has yet to be seriously addressed. A very different approach is needed to nurture culture change... The £30 billion question is not just whether NPfIT will get the technology right but whether it can also win the hearts and minds of the people on whom the NHS depends every day.

Patients are also unhappy about NPfIT, even at this early stage of the project. Most of the patient concerns are directed at the ability of NPfIT to protect records. This distrust is illustrated by a Web site, *http://www.TheBigOptOut.org*, which states,

---

3 "U.K. Dept. of Health: Prescription for Disaster," November 13, 2006, by Laton McCartney.

4 iSOFT Group Interim results for the six months ended October 31, 2006.

This system is designed to be a huge national database of patient medical records and personal information (sometimes referred to as the NHS 'spine') with no opt-out mechanism for patients at all. It is being rolled out during 2007, and is objectionable for many of the same reasons as the government's proposed ID database... You will no longer be able to attend any Sexual Health or GUM (Genito-Urinary Medicine) Clinic anonymously as all these details will also be held on this national database, alongside your medical records. For the first time everyone's most up-to-date and confidential details are to be held on one massive database.

But of all the constituent groups that have expressed unhappiness with NPfIT, the most vocal by far has been the IT community. In January 2005, The British Computer Society (BCS) sent a position paper to the NAO describing a number of concerns with the NPfIT approach, including the following:

- Failure to communicate with health care users
- Monolithic approach
- Stifling of innovation among the health informatics market
- Lack of record confidentiality
- Quality of the shared data

In April 2006, 23 highly respected academicians sent an open letter to the Health Select Committee. In this letter, they made some harsh statements:

Concrete, objective information about NPfIT's progress is not available to external observers. Reliable sources within NPfIT have raised concerns about the technology itself. The National Audit Office report about NPfIT is delayed until this summer, at earliest; the report is not expected to address major technical issues. As computer scientists, engineers and informaticians, we question the wisdom of continuing NPfIT without an independent assessment of its basic technical viability.

In October 2006, this same group sent another open letter to the same committee:

Since then [April] a steady stream of reports have increased our alarm about NPfIT. We support Connecting for Health in their commitment to ensure that the NHS has cost-effective, modern IT systems, and we strongly believe that an independent and constructive technical review in the form that we proposed is an essential step in helping the project to succeed... we believe that there is a compelling case for your committee to conduct an immediate Inquiry: to establish the scale of the risks facing NPfIT; to initiate the technical review; and to identify appropriate shorter-term measures to protect the program's objectives.

The BCS offered to help the NHS with a review of the NPfIT architecture. What did NHS think of this generous offer? Not much. Lord Warner, head of the NHS responded forcefully:

> *"I do not support the call by 23 academics to the House of Commons Health Select Committee to commission a review of the NPfIT's technical architecture. I want the Program's management and suppliers to concentrate on implementation, and not be diverted by attending to another review."*[5]

Soon after, Lord Warner apparently had had enough. Like Accenture, he was bailing out. In December 2006, he announced his retirement from the NHS. He was followed in July 2007 by Richard Granger, Director General of IT for NHS, the man who was widely blamed for most, if not all, of NPfIT's problems.

At this point, nobody knows what the eventual cost for NPfIT will be. Estimates range from $48 billion to $100 billion. It seems likely that the project will go down in history as the world's most expensive IT failure.

The SIP Approach

Clearly, NPfIT is a very expensive project in very deep trouble. But could SIP have helped? Let's look at how the SIP process would have likely played out with NPfIT.

Let's start in Phase 1. The first deliverable of Phase 1 is an audit of organizational readiness. Such an audit would have revealed deep distrust between the NHS IT organization and the business units (health care providers). This would have been an immediate sign of concern.

Also in Phase 1 we would have delivered extensive training in the nature of complexity. We would have spent considerable time discussing how important it was that complexity, especially on such a massive undertaking as NPfIT, be managed as the absolute highest priority.

In Phase 2, we would have been working on the partitioning. In the case of NPfIT, considerable effort had already been done on partitioning; Figure 6-1 could be viewed as an ABC diagram of NPfIT. The question is, does that diagram represent good partitioning? Is it even a partitioning (in the mathematical sense) at all?

Figure 6-1 does not give us enough information to answer this question. We need to understand not only how the organization is being decomposed into sets of functionality, but what the type relationships are between those sets.

So let's tackle this. Figure 6-3 shows an ABC diagram of the clinical information part of NPfIT (the part that owns 80 percent of the NPfIT budget), focusing on types, implementations, and deployments. Compare this figure to Figure 6-1.

---

[5] BJHC.CO.UK, November, 2006.

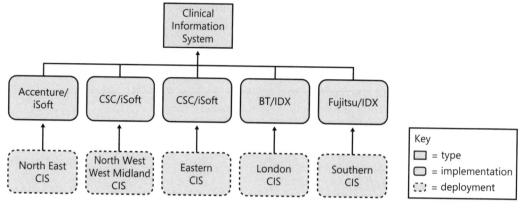

FIGURE 6-3 ABC diagram of NPfIT regional CIS.

In Figure 6-3, the central problem of NPfIT jumps out like a sore thumb (a $10 billion sore thumb). They implemented the various regional clinical information systems as siblings (in SIP talk) rather than as clones. In other words, they created five different implementations of the same system. The same very complex system.

Interestingly, NHS did this on purpose. Now why, you might ask, would anybody take a highly complex system that they would be lucky to implement properly once and tempt the fates with five completely different implementations created by five completely different vendors?

The reason NHS gave for the multiple implementations was that it didn't want to be dependent on any one vendor. This example illustrates a common reason that so many projects become so complex so quickly: poor communication between the business and IT units.

Somebody in the business group decides on some business requirement—say, X. In this case, X can be stated as, "There must be no dependency on any one vendor for the regional CIS portion of NPfIT." X gets passed around. It sounds reasonable. Who wants to be dependent on one vendor? X is accepted as a business requirement. It drives a series of technical requirements. In this case, the technical requirement is that there must five independent implementations of the regional CIS.

Everything seems reasonable. A reasonable business requirement driving the necessary technical requirements. So what would have been done differently using SIP?

A SIP process would have encouraged this business requirement to have been measured against the complexity it would introduce. Complexity, in the SIP world, trumps almost everything. The diagram in Figure 6-3 would have been a warning sign that we have a huge amount of unnecessary complexity. Because both the business and technical folks would have already been through the SIP training, they would understand the frightening implications of complexity. On a project of this scope, the project motto should be, "Our Top Three Concerns: Complexity, Complexity, Complexity."

Given a common conditioned response to complexity, it would have been easy to discuss the importance of this particular business requirement relative to its cost. We would have asked some pointed questions. Is it really necessary to be vendor independent? Is the multibillion dollar cost worth vendor independence? Is meeting this requirement going to put the project at more risk than if we dropped this requirement? Is it even possible to be vendor independent? Are multiple implementations the only way to achieve vendor independence? Would parallel implementations, with one chosen in a final shootout, be a better approach to achieving vendor independence?

I don't know which solution would have been chosen in a SIP approach. But I know one solution that would *not* have been chosen: five independent implementations of the same type. This is an extreme case of an unpartitioned architecture. And an unpartitioned architecture, in a SIP analysis, is unacceptable. It is not unacceptable because one person or another doesn't like the diagrams it produces. It is unacceptable because it fails to satisfy the mathematical models that predict whether or not the architecture can be successful.

So by the end of Phase 2, we would have dropped four of the five proposed implementations for regional clinical information systems. Expected complexity reduction: 80 percent.

But we aren't done yet. Next we enter Phase 3, the phase in which we simplify our partition. I'll continue my focus on the regional CIS portion of NPfIT.

Of course, we have already done quite a bit to simplify the regional CIS portion. We have eliminated 80 percent of the work, but we are still left with a highly complex system. What is the best way to simplify a highly complex system? If you have been following the SIP discussion, the answer should be obvious: partitioning. The most effective way to tame the regional CIS monster is to partition it into four or five subsets, each with synergistic functionality, and each with functionality that is autonomous with respect to the functionality in the other subsets.

One possible partition of subsets might include, for example, patient registration, appointment booking, prescriptions, patient records, and lab and radiology tests.

To explain this in SIP terminology, we have taken an autonomous business capability (ABC) that includes the regional CIS and decomposed it into five lower level ABCs. Figure 6-4 shows the regional CIS ABC before and after this process.

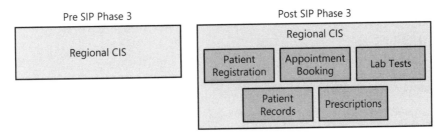

FIGURE 6-4 Decomposition of regional CIS.

At this point, we check our post-SIP analysis against the five Laws of Partitions. The First Law says that all the original functionality of the regional CIS must end up in one and only one of the subsets. The Second Law says that the subsets must make sense from an organizational perspective. The Third Law says that there should be a reasonable number of subsets in the partition. The Fourth Law says that subsets must be roughly equal in size and stature. The Fifth Law says that subset interactions must be minimal and well regulated. The first four laws can be checked relatively easily. The fifth law needs to be revisited after we have more details about the technical architecture.

The partitioning of the regional CIS ABC will likely result in a huge further reduction in complexity. How much? The mathematical models predict possible reductions of more than 99.99 percent. These are based on theoretical numbers, not real-world numbers, but as I discussed in Chapter 3, "Mathematics of Complexity," 90-percent reductions in the real world are likely. And remember, we have already removed 80 percent of the complexity, so now we are removing 90 percent of the 20 percent that is left. This means that realistically we are now down to perhaps 2 percent of the complexity with which we started.

And there is yet more we can do to reduce complexity. We can look at reducing both the functionality footprint (the amount of functionality in the final system) and the implementation footprint (the impact on the IT staff).

Reducing the functionality footprint means re-examining all the business and technical requirements and confirming that, first of all, every business requirement is absolutely necessary, and second of all, that every technical requirement can be traced back to a business requirement. Remember that we have already found one business requirement (vendor dependence) that is either unnecessary or highly suspect.

Reducing the implementation footprint means looking for opportunities to consolidate or outsource subsets. The type information we have generated on the ABCs will be a great help in our efforts to reduce the implementation footprint.

The next phase is Phase 4, in which we prioritize the subsets making up the partition. Again, I will focus on the regional CIS portion of NPfIT.

In Phase 3, we identified five subsets of the regional CIS that together form a partition:

- Patient Registration
- Appointment Booking
- Prescriptions
- Patient Records
- Lab Tests

In the actual NHS plan, this functionality was delivered en masse. In the SIP approach, we want to deliver this functionality iteratively. In Phase 4, we decide on the order of iteration.

Iteration order should be based on risk, cost, and benefit. The basic rule of thumb is to go for the low-hanging fruit first. In the SIP world, low-hanging fruit is defined as ABCs that are highly visible, low cost, and low risk. These requirements are sometimes at odds with each other (although, in my experience, less often than people think). The best way to sort this out is with the Value Graph Analysis that I described in Chapter 5, "SIP Process." If we were using Value Graph Analysis in this project, we would have standardized the analysis back in Phase 1 of the project.

What usually makes an ABC "high visibility" is its association with organizational pain points. Let's say, for example, that NHS was notorious for the length of time it took to book appointments. This factor would tend to move *Appointment Booking* ahead in the priority list. *Lab Tests*, on the other hand, might be something that is already handled reasonably well. Lab Tests might still be worth doing, say, because it can reduce the cost of processing lab tests, but without high visibility, it doesn't rate as a high priority.

Let's say that at the end of Phase 4 we have decided on the following order of iterations:

1. Appointment Booking
2. Patient Registration
3. Prescriptions
4. Patient Records
5. Lab Tests

Next is Phase 5, the iterative phase. As I have said, Phase 5 is the one in which we have the fewest opinions, other than that the candidate ABCs be implemented in an iterative fashion and that the order follow the priority laid out in Phase 4. The implementation of an ABC is effectively a solution architecture and implementation issue, and I'm assuming that an organization already has processes in place to create and implement a solution architecture. You might, for example, use The Open Group Architectural Framework (TOGAF), with its emphasis on process and current and future architectures. You might use some of the Federal Enterprise Architecture (FEA) characterizations of functionality given in its Reference Models. You might use Zachman's taxonomy to ensure that you are considering each important perspective on each important capability of the system. You might use IBM's Unified Process or the Microsoft Solution Framework to guide the implementation process. These are outside of the scope of SIP.

But the iterative approach is not outside the scope of SIP. I believe that the first ABC should be rolled out, tested, approved, deployed, and embraced before the next one is started. Such an approach allows you to learn your lessons as cheaply as possible and apply them as broadly as possible. It also helps you build enthusiasm for the overall project. Nothing succeeds, as they say, like success. Success attracts success. Let's see how such an approach might have benefited NPfIT. We could look at any number of issues plaguing NPfIT. Let's consider one that I haven't discussed yet: risk management.

LORENZO was an existing product developed by iSOFT, and NHS was impressed with LORENZO's user-friendly screens and broad CIS functionality. For this reason, NHS encouraged its use as a core component for all of its regional CIS systems.

Accenture seemed similarly impressed with LORENZO. In June 2004, Accenture/iSOFT released a joint press release saying,

> *A set of information processing tools promoting governance, quality, efficiency, and consent in healthcare, LORENZO facilitates the free flow of information among the entire healthcare community, including general practitioners, hospitals and patients. As Accenture deploys LORENZO across the two regions, the software's unified architecture will form the basis of solutions tailored to meet local requirements and information needs of healthcare professionals.*[6]

But there was a hidden time bomb in LORENZO. This time bomb can be summed up in two words: client/server.

According to a performance audit of LORENZO conducted in April 2006 by Health Industry Insights and commissioned by iSOFT, the LORENZO architecture as it existed in 2004 was "based on a fat client/server model."[7] Accenture was either blissfully unaware of the fact that LORENZO was a client/server system or was ignorant of the issues one faces with client/server architectures.

What is the problem with client/server models? The client/server architecture is based on a two-machine configuration. One machine (the "client") contains the user-interface code and the business logic. The other machine (the "server") contains the code that manages data in the database.

The two machines are "connected" by database connections. A database connection is created when a client machine requests access rights to the database owned by the server. The database looks at the credentials of the requesting machine, and, if it is satisfied, creates a database connection. A database connection is technically a block of data that the client presents to the server machine when making data access requests. When the client machine is ready to shut down for the day, it releases its database connection by letting the server machine know that it will no longer require the services of the database.

There are several reasons that client/server architectures are so popular. For one, they are very fast. They are fast because the client machine requests the database connection (a highly expensive request) only once, in the beginning of the day, when the client machine is first started.

---

[6] "iSOFT Delivers LORENZO for Deployment," Accenture, June 16, 2004.

[7] "Coming of Age: A Report on a Performance Benchmark Test of iSOFT's LORENZO Clinical Information System," by Marc Holland and Luisa Bordoni, April 2006.

Client/server systems are also easy to implement because the code that presents the data (the "user interface logic") is located in the same process as the code that manipulates the data (the "business logic"). This makes it easy to mingle the presentation logic and the business logic, with the result of lightning-fast data presentation and manipulation.

So back to my original question. What is wrong with a client/server architecture? Actually, there is only one problem with client/server systems. They do not scale. Although they work great for small numbers of users (measured, say, in the dozens), they do not work at all well for large numbers of users (measured, say, in the thousands). And the user requirements of NPfIT were measured in the tens of thousands.

The reason client/server architectures do not scale well is that each client machine requires a dedicated database connection. Databases are limited in the number of database connections they can support. When each client requires a dedicated database connection, the number of client machines is limited by the number of database connections supported by the database. And because client machines are in a one-to-one relationship to users, this limits the number of users who can use the system at any one time.

So a client/server architecture, with its extreme limitation on numbers of clients, is a problem for NPfIT. A big problem.

To address the scalability limitations of client/server architectures, a new style of technical architecture was developed, initially, in the 1970s, and was quite mature by the mid-1980s. This new style of technical architecture is known as three-tier.

In a three-tier architecture, one machine runs the database, as it had in the client/server architecture. But now the user-interface logic and the business logic are separated. The user-interface logic lives on the machine before which the human being sits. But the business logic lives on another machine. This machine is often referred to as the "middle tier" because it conceptually lives in between the user interface machine and the database machine.

It is the middle tier machine that owns the database connections. This arrangement allows a pooling of those very expensive database connections so that when a database connection is not being used by one client, it can be used by another.

So the obvious issue that iSOFT faced with its LORENZO product, back in 2004, was how to take a product based on a fundamentally nonscalable architecture and turn it into a scalable system. There is really only one answer to this problem. The company had to rearchitect LORENZO from a client/server architecture to some variation of a three-tier architecture.

This, according to that previously quoted audit, is exactly what iSOFT did. In fact, the company decided that it would go one better. It would bypass the three-tier architecture and move directly to an even more advanced architecture known as service-oriented architecture (SOA). An SOA is essentially an architecture in which the middle tier has been split further apart, with business functionality distributed over a number of middle-tier-like machines, each using industry-standard service-oriented messages as a communications protocol.

As the audit stated,

> this new [LORENZO] architecture... utilizes a service oriented architecture (SOA) ...
> making iSOFT the first major CIS vendor worldwide to base its overall architecture
> principally on SOA. This architecture will serve as the foundation for the entire line
> of LORENZO solutions, allowing different subsets or combinations of existing and
> planned functional capabilities to be delivered on a common technical platform. For
> both iSOFT and its clients, this strategy will facilitate the ability to cost-effectively
> configure and scale CIS applications to meet a wide range of organizational models
> and functional demands...because the client machine is almost entirely focused on
> working with the human client.

Although this transformation from client/server to SOA was absolutely necessary from a scalability perspective, it was also something else: highly risky.

Many organizations have "ported" three-tier architectures to SOAs. This process is usually straightforward because the two architectures are so similar. However, LORENZO, remember, was not a three-tier architecture. It was a client/server architecture.

The transformation from client/server to either three-tier or SOA is rarely straightforward. Either process requires massive changes to the underlying programs. All of that nicely intermingled user-interface and business logic needs to be painstakingly located and laboriously separated. More often than not, it is less expensive to re-implement the system from scratch rather than try to make (and debug) the necessary changes. So while LORENZO might have been a wonderful product, it was a product that would have to be rewritten from the ground up to meet the needs of NPfIT. And further, it would need to be rewritten by a group that had no previous experience in either three-tier architectures or SOAs, both of which are highly specialized areas.

There is no way to know if Accenture knew about this high-risk factor back in 2004. It should have. Any reasonably competent architect could have looked at the LORENZO code and recognized the unmistakable fingerprint of a client/server architecture. But there was no indication in its joint press release that this issue was understood or that the risk factor had been addressed.

The indications are that by the time the limitations of LORENZO's architecture were understood, three of the five regional clusters of NPfIT were in serious trouble and Accenture was so deeply over its head that it was ready to jump from the sinking ship.

An iterative approach to delivering the regions would not have made the iSOFT architectural limitations any less real. But it would have made them obvious much earlier in the project. While it might have been too late to save all three regions that had bet on LORENZO, at least two of the regions could have learned from the painful lessons of the first. Billions of dollars would likely have been saved overall.

Iterative delivery is a key strategy in managing high-risk factors. Unfortunately, it is a strategy that was not used by NPfIT.

There is yet another problem facing NPfIT besides risky architectures, and this is low user confidence. Let's see how this played out in NPfIT and how iteration could have helped.

Regardless of how good or bad NPfIT ends up, its ultimate success or failure is in the hands of its users. The support of the hundreds of thousands of health care workers and patients will determine the final judgment of this project. As with most large IT projects, user perception *is* reality. If users think the project is a success, it is a success. If users think the project is a failure, it is a failure, regardless of how much the project owners believe otherwise.

Iterative delivery can be a great help here. If the early deliveries are a failure, their failures are limited in scope and in visibility. If they are a success, the enthusiasm of the initial users becomes contagious. Everybody wants to be the next owner of the new toy!

As I pointed out earlier in this chapter, NPfIT suffers a major credibility gap with health care workers, patients, and the IT community. It seems that nobody other than NHS management believes that this multibillion dollar investment is going to pay off.

Could it have been different? Suppose NHS had chosen the highest visibility ABC from the list of candidates, the *Appointment Booking* ABC. Imagine that NHS had endured years of criticism for difficulties in its current booking procedures and then rolled out this new automated booking system. Suppose it first showed prototypes to the health care professionals. Say they loved the interface but had a few suggestions. NHS then incorporated those suggestions and rolled out the Appointment Booking to one region.

Very quickly booking in that region went from six-month waiting lists to four-day waiting lists. Appointments that used to require hours of standing in line now take a few minutes on a Web browser or on a phone. Other regions would be clamoring to be the next one in line for deployment.

As Appointment Booking was deployed across the UK, the entire health care system would have appeared to have been transformed. Even though only one small part of the overall health care process, appointments, had been affected, that impact would have been felt in a positive way by every constituent group.

As NHS started work on its next ABC, Patient Registration, it would be basking in the success of its previous work. It would be facing a world that supported its efforts, believed its promises, and eagerly awaited its next delivery.

This is the way it could have been had NHS used an iterative delivery model based on SIP. But it didn't. And instead, it faces a world that ridicules its efforts, laughs at its promises, and dreads its next delivery. The world believes that NPfIT will be a failure. In the eyes of the world, failure is all NHS has delivered. Why should the future be any different?

Ironically, even if NPfIT does manage to deliver any successes, it will be hard pressed to prove it. Why? Because at the start of this multibillion dollar project, nobody bothered to document what success would look like in any measurable fashion. Let me show you what I mean.

The NPfIT business plan of 2005[8] gave these success indicators for patients:

- Patients will have a greater opportunity to influence the way they are treated by the NHS.

- Patients will be able to discuss their treatment options and experience a more personalised health service.

- Patients will experience greater convenience and certainty, which will reduce the stress of referral.

- Patients will have a choice of time and place, which will enable them to fit their treatment in with their life, not the other way round.

For health care providers, the business plan promised these benefits:

- General practitioners and their practice staff will have much greater access to their patients' care management plans, ensuring that the correct appointments are made.

- General practitioners and practice staff will see a reduction in the amount of time spent on the paper chase and bureaucracy associated with existing referral processes.

- Consultants and booking staff will see a reduction in the administrative burden of chasing hospital appointments on behalf of patients.

- The volume of Did Not Attends (DNAs) will reduce, because patients will agree on their date, and consultants will have a more secure referral audit trail.

What do all of these deliverables have in common? None have any yardstick that can be used to measure success or failure. None are attached to any dollar amount that can help justify the project. In fact, one could argue that all of these "success factors" could have been met by simply replacing the manual pencil sharpeners by electric ones!

I made the assertion in Chapter 5 that while many organizations claim to use an ROI (return on investment) yardstick to justify new projects, few really do. NPfIT is an excellent example of this. There is not a single ROI measurable included in the so-called success factors.

SIP is dogmatic about the need for measurable success factors tied to dollar amounts. It is a critical part of the prioritization activity of Phase 4 and is made concrete in the Value Graph Analysis. What would SIP-mandated measurable success factors have looked like? Here are some possible examples:

- A reduction by 50 percent in the personnel hours spent managing patient booking. This will save 140 million person hours per year at a savings of approximately $1.56 billion annually.

- A reduction by 50 percent of the DNAs (Did Not Attends), for a savings of $780 million annually.

---

8   NHS Business Plan 2005/2006.

- A reduction by 75 percent of the cost of managing patient records, for a savings of $3.50 billion annually.

Do these specific measurables make sense? They are at least consistent with the NHS released data. I have no way to know if they are accurate or not, but these are the kind of measurements that would have served two purposes. First, they would have allowed the NHS to determine if it had, in fact, met its goals once (or if) NPfIT is ever completed. Second, they could have been used to convince a skeptical public that the project was worth undertaking in the first place.

NHS is in the process of learning a very expensive, very painful lesson. Complexity is your enemy. Control it, or it will control you.

Summary

In this chapter, I looked at a system called NPfIT (National Program for Information Technology). This system shares three characteristics with many other IT systems:

1. It is highly complex.
2. It is very expensive.
3. It is headed down a path of failure.

The lessons we can learn by examining NPfIT can help us avoid similar problems in other large projects. We saw how the features of SIP could have helped control the complexity of this massive project and, by extension, can be used to avoid similar problems in other projects.

SIP's obsession with complexity control would have helped bring sanity to a discussion of the business requirements of NPfIT. SIP's partitioning could have pinpointed areas of extreme complexity very early in the project. SIP's simplification could have removed as much as 98 percent of the project's complexity, and possibly more. SIP's iteration could have highlighted risks early in the project, where they could have been corrected easily and helped transform a world of skeptics to a world of supporters.

If SIP could do all of this for a project of the complexity of NPfIT, what can it do for your project?

Chapter 7
Guarding the Boundaries: Software Fortresses

Autonomous business capabilities (ABCs) represent optimal subsets of functionality within an organization. ABCs logically contain both the business processes and the technical systems that together deliver the ABCs functionality.

We know that ABCs need to interact. In simple iterative partitions (SIP), this interaction is referred to as *partner relationships*. I have discussed the concern about partner relationships: they represent the thin spots between ABCs—that is, places where the boundaries between partitions are likely to be compromised.

An ABC is an equivalence class, or subset, of a larger partition. The rules of partitions state that a subset is part of a partition if the elements living inside that subset are independent of the elements living inside other subsets of that partition. Stating this in SIP terms, the functionality in an ABC must be independent (or autonomous) of the functionality in any other ABC.

So we see a conflict here. On the one hand, ABCs must interact. On the other hand, interactions between ABCs compromise the partition. And any compromises to the partition compromise our efforts toward simplification. How do we achieve reasonable interaction between ABCs without watching our effort toward simplification slip away?

The interaction between ABCs can occur either through interaction of the business processes or the IT systems of the ABC. In practice, the trend is for interaction to occur primarily between the IT systems. This trend is accelerating as the world embraces technologies such as shared databases, service-oriented architectures (SOAs), and software-as-a-service. How do we take advantage of these technologies without relinquishing our commitments to simple architectures? This is the question I will explore in this chapter.

Technical Partitions

First, let's explore what it means for two ABCs to be technically independent of each other. Here is my test for technical independence. Two systems—say, A and B—are technically 100-percent independent of each other if any and all lines of code in system A could be arbitrarily changed without having an impact on system B, and vice versa.

Let's look at some common approaches to interoperability between A and B and see how each approach does on the independence test.

If systems A and B are both in the same process, one of the most common approaches to interoperability is to make direct procedure calls (for procedural style code) or method invocations (for object-oriented code) from A to B and vice versa. This approach is shown in Figure 7-1.

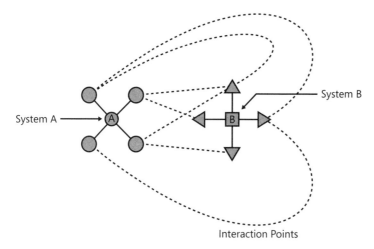

System A

System B

Interaction Points

FIGURE 7-1 Interoperability through procedure call/method invocation.

As Figure 7-1 shows, interoperability through procedure call or method invocation typically involves a large number of access points, each of which contain potentially large amounts of code. The code in these access points represents mutual dependency between the two systems. If any of these change in system A, then system B will fail and vice versa.

This approach yields a low degree of independence (or, equivalently, high dependence). This is bad. On a scale of 1 to 10, where 1 is low independence and 10 is high independence, I rate this a 1.

A second approach to interoperability is to use shared databases. In this approach, systems A and B share access to the same underlying database. Changes made to the database by system A can be seen by system B and vice versa. This approach is shown in Figure 7-2.

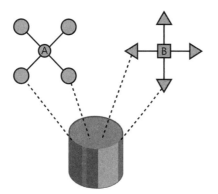

FIGURE 7-2 Interoperability through a shared database.

When achieving interoperability through shared databases, there are fewer connection points between the two systems than with interoperability through direct function/method invocations. There are still dependencies, but the dependencies are limited to the code that reads from and writes to the database. As long as system A doesn't change how it accesses the database, the rest of the code can be changed without having an impact on system B and vice versa. I rate this approach a 5 (fair) on the scale of independence.

A third approach to interoperability involves the use of a shared data access layer. In this approach, systems A and B agree to use the same data access layer to get to the database. The data access layer translates business entities, such as customers, into database entities, such as rows and columns. This approach is shown in Figure 7-3.

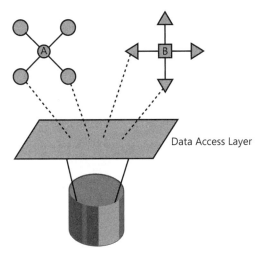

FIGURE 7-3 Interoperability through a shared data access layer.

Interoperability through a shared data access layer is similar to interoperability through shared databases. Theoretically, fewer lines are involved because the data access layer delivers business objects to the systems, bypassing the need to translate. The main drawback is that all or most systems in an enterprise must agree to use this data access layer. This requires an enterprise-wide consensus on what that data access layer will look like. In my experience, both the agreement and the consensus are difficult to achieve. I would rate this as a 6 (slightly better than fair) on the scale of independence.

An increasingly common approach to interoperability is to use service-oriented architectures (SOAs). The term SOA is not well defined, but I will use it in its narrowest possible sense—namely, that two systems interoperate through the use of communications protocols based on Web-service standards. In the most common variant of this approach, some number of object-oriented methods in systems A and B are wrapped as Web services. Systems A and B can then make requests of each other through these services. This approach is shown in Figure 7-4.

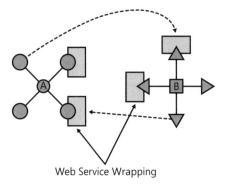

Web Service Wrapping

FIGURE 7-4 Interoperability through an SOA.

Interoperability through SOAs is somewhat similar to the shared data access layer approach because both require a consensus on what the wrapping layer looks like. The main difference is that for SOAs some consensus has already been reached. The industry has agreed on a number of Web-service standards to define this layer, the best known of which is Simple Object Access Protocol (SOAP). Web-service standards define only how messages will be transmitted between the two systems. Consensus still needs to be reached in the enterprise on the nature of the messages that will go back and forth between the systems. This consensus is usually easier to achieve than resolving the contentious discussions that occur over data access layers. I rate this an 8 on the scale of independence.

Although the SOA approach to interoperability is the best of the common approaches, it still has problems. For example, if system A decides to change the character of the messages it will accept, system B's communication links with A will be broken. If A decides to start using more of the Web-service standards—such as security, reliable messaging, or transactional support—these changes will almost certainly break B's communication links. If B finds some back door into A—say, through accessing a common database—the back door can greatly decrease the independence of the two systems.

To solve these problems with SOAs, I advocate another approach to interoperability. I call this approach the *software fortress* approach. The software fortress approach to interoperability advocates the use of SOAs, but only within well-defined architectural constraints. The software fortress approach maximizes interoperability while minimizing the breakdown in partition boundaries between the two systems. From a SIP perspective, this model enables ABC partner relationships while still maintaining the best possible partition boundaries. Or to put it another way, it minimizes the thin spots between partners.

In the software fortress model, no part of system A is wrapped with a Web service. Instead, an outside entity, called a *guard* is implemented with Web services. This guard then interacts with system A on behalf of the outside system—say, system B. This model is shown in Figure 7-5.

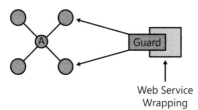

FIGURE 7-5 Use of a guard.

The guard accepts the incoming message on behalf of system A. On the outgoing side (system B), there is an analogous entity to the guard that creates and sends messages. This entity is called an *envoy*. The envoy is wrapped with whatever Web-service standards are needed to send messages. When system B wants to communicate with system A, it communicates this request to its envoy. The envoy creates a Web-service message and sends it to the guard. The guard receives the message and communicates it to system A. This transfer is shown in Figure 7-6.

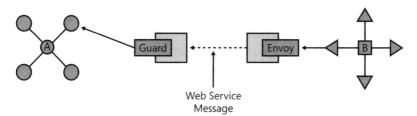

FIGURE 7-6 Transfer of a message in the software fortress model.

The advantage of using guards and envoys is that they protect the actual systems from any changes in how the Web services are being used. If system A decides to start using the security standards and requires, for example, encryption of messages, it is only the envoy on the system B side that needs to be modified.

However, there is still the issue of back doors. To ensure that nobody is accessing system A in any way other than through approved channels (the guard), *walls* are constructed around the systems with *portals* for approved communications. These walls are typically constructed using a combination of firewalls, role-based access, and database security. Figure 7-7 shows the addition of the walls and portals to the software fortress model.

This software fortress then encapsulates the software for a given ABC. The rules of the fortress must therefore be consistent with the rules of partitioning. I'll take you through these next.

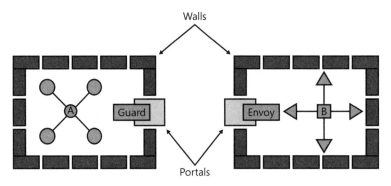

FIGURE 7-7 The software fortress model with walls.

Rule 1: Autonomy

Rule 1 is that the software system inside the fortress is autonomous with respect to outside systems. This is, of course, a requirement of partitioning and a natural byproduct of using the equivalence relation *synergistic* to construct the ABC in the first place. Something that is autonomous is self-reliant and exists as an independent body. It is free of outside constraints and able to act of its own free will. For a fortress, this means that it can provide some significant piece of business functionality and that it is independent of outside systems to provide that functionality.

Autonomy is not only a technical concept, but usually an organizational one, too. A given fortress—say, CreditCardAuthorization—is typically built by a small group of people (probably fewer than 10) who work closely together, make decisions together, and are independent of outside groups to complete their work. The group that developed the CreditCardAuthorization fortress is probably different from the group that developed the Shipping fortress.

Autonomy is often a gray area. Shipping might be dependent on CreditCardAuthorization to processes credit cards. The test of autonomy becomes whether or not the Shipping service provides value *by itself*, without the help of the outside system(s). If we didn't have credit card processing systems, for example, the Shipping service would still have value. It just has more value when it can ship items that were purchased with credit cards. The deciding test is that of synergy. Remember that autonomy is the inverse equivalence relation to synergy.

Rule 2: Explicit Boundaries

Rule 2 is that the fortress boundaries are explicit. We know exactly when we are inside the fortress and when we are outside. We expect to undergo technology phase shifts as we move from one side of the boundary to the other. For example, inside the fortress, distributed communications typically use native distributed communications protocols. Once that communication prepares to leave the fortress, it is translated into a SOAP request by the envoy. When the SOAP request is received by the guard, it is translated back into a native communications protocol. Phase shifts are processed by the guard and the envoy.

Rule 3: Partitioning of Functionality

Rule 3 says that an enterprise's collection of services should form a functionality partition. This means that a given piece of business functionality must exist in one and only one fortress. This failure to partition was one of the reasons the National Program for Information Technology (NPfIT) system discussed in Chapter 6, "A Case Study in Complexity," was so complex. There were five different implementations for booking a patient, depending on the location of the patient. This arrangement is a violation of the mathematical principles of partitioning, which state that every element of the universe must live in one and only one subset of the universe.

Rule 4: Dependencies Defined by Policy

Rule 4 states that all dependencies between two fortresses are defined by policy. *Policy* is a catch-all phrase that includes the definitions of the communications between the envoy (on the outgoing side) and the guard (on the incoming side). Policy includes information about the schema (message formats), transport (message channels), contract (message sequences), and context (message envelopes). Policy does not include information about what happens prior to the envoy sending the message or after the guard receives the message. In the software fortress model, nobody sees this interfortress message except the envoy and the guard.

Policy is limited to descriptions of the communications between the envoy and the guard. Because the envoy and the guard are not strictly part of the two systems, this rule also states that there are no dependencies between two systems that live in different ABCs (and, therefore, fortresses). Thus, this rule indirectly states that there can be no back doors and no shared databases—nothing that would serve to weaken the boundaries separating the two ABCs.

Rule 5: Asynchronicity

Rule 5 says that all communication between fortresses must be done asynchronously. This is quite different from how most Web-service communication is done today. Although the Web-service standards support both synchronous and asynchronous communications, synchronous communications is the norm. The reason for this is that most programmers are very familiar with synchronous communications and have very little experience with asynchronous communications.

In synchronous communications, the sender sends a message to the receiver and then blocks until the receiver replies. This approach introduces a block in the sender over which the sender has no control. It also introduces a time dependency in the logic of the sender. It cannot complete until the sender replies. Time dependencies are not specified in policy, thus synchronous communications is a violation of Rule 4, which states that all dependencies must be limited to those specified in policy.

Asynchronous messages work differently. When A sends B a message, there is no built-in assumption about when that message will be delivered. When B gets the message, it will act. In the meantime, A can continue with whatever it would like to do.

There are actually many other reasons for insisting on asynchronous communications between fortresses. These reasons would literally fill a book. Asynchronous communications not only eliminates time blocks, it also results in more scalable, more reliable, and less expensive systems. But these issues are beyond the scope of this present discussion. Suffice it to say that the use of asynchronous communications between fortresses will provide many indirect benefits to the information technology (IT) systems that make up the ABC.

In the real world, I do not believe that literally all interfortress communications can be done asynchronously. There are some situations that seem to require synchronous communications. Still, I believe synchronous communications should be the exception, not the rule.

Rule 6: Partitioning of Data

Rule 6 says that an enterprise's collection of information should form a data partition. This means that any given piece of data is owned by one and seen by only one fortress. For example, credit card information is owned by a CreditCardAuthorization fortress and cannot be seen directly by a Shipping fortress. The CreditCardAuthorization fortress is similarly oblivious to how Shipping stores its addresses.

This idea will seem very controversial to many. It implies, for one thing, that enterprise data stores are passé. This rule has tremendous implications regarding how data is managed.

Although Rule 6 will scandalize many, it is, in fact, a natural corollary of Rule 4 (dependencies are defined only by policy). If two fortresses share data, a change on the part of one fortress's management of data will have an impact on the other fortress. This scenario implies that the second fortress is dependent on how the first stores data. But Rule 4 states that the two fortresses can have no dependencies other than those specified in policy. Policy has no information about data storage. Thus, sharing data violates Rule 4.

Some people try to get around this rule by using a shared data access layer, a technique I discussed earlier in this chapter. However, the use of a shared data access layer implies that the second fortress is dependent on the first fortress's willingness to use the shared data access. This, too, is a dependency that is outside of the policy. Thus it, too, violates Rule 4.

Rule 7: No Cross-Fortress Transactions

Business requirements often put some constraints on the relationships between ABCs and thus between fortresses. Take, for example, the retail system discussed in Rule 1. Clearly, we don't want to ship the goods the customer ordered if the CreditCardAuthorization service declines the card. So there is a business dependency between Shipping and CreditCardAuthorization that will translate into some technical dependency. The goal is to introduce the absolute minimal technical dependency that meets the business requirements of no-authorization/no-ship.

There are at least three technical solutions to this functional dependency. Let's briefly consider each.

The first alternative is to use a *synchronous* request. We could have the Sales service make a synchronous call to the CreditCardAuthorization service and wait for the authorization before proceeding to the Shipping service. If the authorization fails, the shipping request never gets made. As I discussed in Rule 5, this is unacceptable or at least undesirable.

The second alternative is to use a *transaction*. We could have the credit authorization done inside the same database transaction as the shipping. Then if the credit authorization fails, Sales can roll back the whole transaction so that the shipping request is undone. The Web-service specifications allow for transactions to span services, and many database programmers consider this an attractive approach.

At the database level, a transaction requires that any database lock held by Sales must continue to be held until CreditCardAuthorization completes its work. Now, not only is the workflow for this order blocked, but any workflow that requires overlapping database activity is also blocked. Technically, this is a very tight dependency. Not only does it require that both fortresses use the same database (a violation of Rule 6), but it introduces a tight dependency that is not covered by policy (a violation of Rule 4).

It is not that I am opposed to transactions. It is only that I am opposed to the transaction crossing the explicit boundary (see Rule 2) of the fortress. Transactions are good. Cross-fortress transactions are bad.

The acceptable alternative to cross-fortress transactions is to use a *business activity*, often called a *compensatory transaction*. Don't mistake the term *compensatory transaction* for *transaction*; the two have nothing to do with one another. With a business activity, we can have Sales make asynchronous requests to both CreditCardAuthorization and Shipping and then use a business activity coordinator to ensure that shipping is not finalized until the credit authorization is completed. The business activity coordinator requires no blocking, no database locks, and no nonpolicy dependencies, and it is compatible with asynchronous communications. It is the coordination strategy of choice for work that involves multiple fortresses.

Rule 8: Single-Point Security

People worry a lot about security. When you are using Web services to access systems, this worry is well founded. Frequently, people address this concern by building in too much security. "Too much security?" you might ask. Isn't that like too much chocolate cake? How can you have too much security?

The problem with security is that it is very tricky. Few developers or architects have the experience to understand the many issues surrounding security. You are better off having less security that is well done than more security that is poorly done. The software fortress model gives you an ideal location to focus your security efforts: the guard. It is the one point through which any outside requests must traverse. By putting all your security here, you can take the few security experts you have and let them focus their activity in the one spot that will be leveraged by all the fortress code.

Rule 9: Inside Trust

Who do you trust? Many processes might be trying to access your fortress, the database your fortress uses, or both. How do you know which ones to trust?

The rule of thumb that I have found works well is to trust every process that runs as part of the fortress (and, therefore, part of the ABC). This means that the database can be configured to give minimally regulated access to all processes in the fortress. You can give wide latitude to processes inside the fortress to communicate freely back and forth.

So who do you not trust? Everybody else. In general, the fortress boundary should also be considered a trust boundary. Inside the fortress, all the implementation details, including processes and databases, trust each other. Anybody outside the fortress is regarded as an intruder.

How do you know which processes outside the fortress are friendly and which aren't? If you are a process that is part of the ABC, you don't know. That is why you force all such requests to go through the guard.

The guidelines, then, are this: Make sure your walls are keeping intruders out. Make sure your guards are letting only friendly requests in. And once the requests are inside, relax.

Rule 10: Keep It Simple

The driving goal of SIP is to reduce complexity. Unfortunately, for many organizations, the drive toward service-orientation does exactly the opposite. Some developers feel that the more flexibility they allow, the better their service/fortress will be. This philosophy translates to creating too many ways to access the functionality, most of which will never be used.

Access points should be created to solve a business problem. They should not be created because some developer wants to be challenged.

The policies that define communications between ABCs should serve a specific business purpose. That purpose should be validated at the enterprise level. Developers who are implementing a fortress often have trouble seeing the perspective of the enterprise. So although the implementation of fortresses should be seen as an independent activity, the policies that define the partner relationships of the fortress should be seen as an enterprise-wide decision and owned by the enterprise architecture team.

Summary

The software fortress model is the basic model that I recommend for implementing the software side of the ABC. It is a model that maximizes opportunities for partner relationships while minimizing the destructive effects of violating the laws of partitions.

There are several important software artifacts that are related to software fortresses. The *walls* prevent unauthorized access to the fortress. The *portals* act as approved entry points. The *guards* make sure that only authorized requests pass through the portals. And *envoys* create and send messages to other fortresses. Software fortresses dovetail nicely with service-oriented architectures, which define the standards used to communicate between envoys and guards.

This chapter presented the 10 rules for software fortresses, many of which are analogous to the laws of partitioning. The 10 rules for software fortresses are as follows:

1. Software fortresses are autonomous with respect to each other.
2. The boundaries of software fortresses are explicit and involve multiple technical phase shifts.
3. Functionality is partitioned among the collection of software fortresses, just as it is among the ABCs making up the enterprise partition.
4. Dependencies between fortresses are limited to information about the messages passing between the envoys and the guards.
5. Messages between fortresses should be sent asynchronously.
6. There should be no overlap between data ownership among fortresses.
7. Tightly coupled database transactions should not cross fortress boundaries.
8. The guards provide the single point of security for the fortress.
9. The fortress boundary serves as a trust boundary.
10. Like everything in the SIP world, keep 'em simple.

Chapter 8
The Path Forward

In December 2007, *CIO Magazine* surveyed 250 Chief Information Officers (CIOs) from a variety of businesses and asked them what their top 10 priorities were for 2008. The results of this survey were nothing short of depressing. The reason is simple: the top seven of the 10 priorities are all fundamentally misguided. The chances of successfully addressing any of these issues using current approaches have virtually no chance of success.

What are these doomed priorities? According to *CIO Magazine,* the number one priority is "Improving alignment with business objectives." This was mentioned by 60 percent of all CIOs (which was almost twice as much as the next most mentioned priority). Ironically, this is the goal that these CIOs have the least chance of meeting. But the next six priorities will fare little better. Here they are, from highest priority to lowest:

- Improving Information Technology (IT) Planning Processes
- Improving Project Management Capabilities
- Reducing IT Costs
- Improving the Return on Investment (ROI) on IT Spending
- Improving Leadership and Management Capabilities
- Improving Systems-Development Capabilities

Why am I so pessimistic about the CIOs' chances of success in any of these seven areas? First of all, we have no historical reason to assume that CIOs know how to solve these problems. For over a decade, CIOs have been attempting to address these exact same issues, and they have yet to find any approaches that work. Whether you are reading this book in 2008, 2009, 2010, or beyond, most CIOs will still be grappling with these same issues.

What are CIOs doing wrong? They are attacking these issues as if they are the fundamental IT problem. These issues are not the problem. They are merely symptoms. It is like trying to cure the flu by providing the patient with facial tissues.

So, for example, these CIOs are attacking the generally poor alignment between IT and the business by trying to coax more information about business needs from their organization and then trying to beat the IT organization into submitting to these needs. But poor IT/business alignment is not the problem. It is only a symptom of the problem. And that same problem is hampering project planning, escalating IT costs, throttling IT ROI, challenging leadership skills, and shackling the ability to plan for systems development.

Complexity: The Real Enemy

The real problem is complexity. As long as complexity continues to run rampant, IT/business alignment will never be possible. Nor will any of these other issues be properly addressed.

That is the bad news. The good news is that if complexity *is* controlled, all of these problems will be suddenly manageable.

That is why the ideas presented in this book are so important. Yes, managing complexity is important, but the reason controlling complexity is so important is because of the problems that uncontrolled complexity creates. Once you control complexity, IT/business alignment falls into place, IT costs are brought under control, IT ROI becomes real and measurable, IT leadership once again becomes a valuable corporate asset, and system planning becomes a routine exercise.

How can I be sure that all of these CIO concerns are so closely related to complexity? It is simple mathematics. Let's look at the number one concern of the CIOs: IT/business alignment.

Imagine that you have a bowl of 14 dice. Seven of the dice are green. These dice represent your business processes. Seven of the dice are red. These dice represent your IT processes. The goal of achieving business/IT alignment can be envisioned as mathematically similar to getting all the dice to come up with the same number. If you shake the bowl, and all the dice come up, say, as ones, then you win. If they don't, you lose.

Let's say that it takes about 10 seconds to shake the bowl, wait for the dice to settle down, and make note of whether you have (or haven't) achieved business/IT alignment. How long will it take to achieve alignment?

Assuming that you do not break for meals, sleeping, or vacations, it will take you, on average, well over 24,000 years to achieve alignment (24,849.11 years, to be exact).

But suppose you organize the dice slightly differently. Instead of putting all the dice in one bowl, let's put the dice in seven bowls, each containing one green dice and one red dice. Now how long will it take to achieve alignment?

Each bowl has 36 possibilities. If it again takes 10 seconds to shake, rattle, and roll, then it will take, on average, 360 seconds to get one of these seven bowls into alignment. But, of course, we don't have one bowl, we have seven, so it will taken 42 minutes (7×360 seconds) to get all the bowls into alignment.

This result is amazing, almost miraculous. By splitting up our 14 dice into seven bowls, we have reduced the time necessary to get the dice into alignment from over 24,000 years to less than one hour. And we have done this without removing or changing any of the dice. The only thing we have done is change how the dice are organized. We have used partitioning.

This lesson is critical to understanding how to better achieve IT/business alignment. The solution is to partition the overall enterprise into a number of smaller subsets, and then, within these subsets, to align the systems. Partitioning dramatically reduces complexity, and once complexity in under control, the alignment problem becomes straightforward. This is the fundamental process of SIP.

This same analysis applies, with minor variations, to all of the top seven CIO concerns. Let's take one more—say, IT costs. IT costs are also directly related to complexity. The more complex a system is, the more it costs to build that system and the more it costs to maintain that system. If system B is twice as complex as system A, it will likely cost twice as much to build and maintain B as A.

How do we make an IT system less complex? Partition it. An IT system represented by eight red dice in one bowl has more than 1,500,000 permutations. Split those dice into four bowls of two dice each and you reduce the number of permutations to 144. That is a huge reduction in complexity and a huge reduction in IT costs.

Partitioning is not just a theoretical concept. It is real. This book has shown you how to do this. If you follow the approach outlined in this book, you will be well on your way to controlling the complexity that is most likely choking your enterprise.

I said earlier that CIOs will still be struggling for the foreseeable future to address the same issues as they are today. There is one group of CIOs for whom I hope this will not be true. That is the group that will have read this book and taken its message to heart.

Simplicity Pays

It is not just the concerns of the CIO that can be better realized by controlling complexity. It is also the concerns of the solution architect. Let me give you an example that shows some of the solution benefits that a simple architecture has over a complex one. This example comes from my workshop on controlling architectural complexity. This workshop is typically attended by representatives from both business and IT, and I like this particular example because it seems to crystallize in many people's minds the business value of simplicity.

In the workshop, I give participants the problem of designing an interlibrary loan system. The high-level ABCs representing the participants are shown in Figure 8-1.

FIGURE 8-1 ABCs of interlibrary loan system.

The three ABCs shown in Figure 8-1 will be in partner relationships with each other. Recall from Chapter 4, "The ABCs of Enterprise Partitions," that ABCs that are in a partner relationship will need to interoperate. The problem I pose to the workshop attendees is to take 20 minutes and design at a high level the communications patterns that will unfold in these two scenarios:

- **Scenario one**   The Austin library decides to purchase a new copy of Shakespeare's *Romeo and Juliet*.

- **Scenario two**   The Houston library wants to borrow a copy of Shakespeare's *Romeo and Juliet* from some library.

Now before you look at either the student solution or my solution, I suggest that you take 20 minutes to try to come up with your own solution to this problem.

Are you ready? OK. When given this problem, most workshop participants come back with some variant on the communications patterns shown in Figure 8-2.

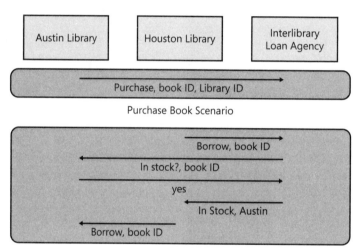

FIGURE 8-2 Typical interlibrary loan architecture.

In the solution shown in Figure 8-2, libraries inform the Interlibrary Loan Agency whenever they purchase a new book. When a library wants to borrow a book on interlibrary loan, that library goes to the agency to find out which library has the book. The agency then checks to see which library has the book, double-checks with that library, and lets the borrowing library know where to borrow the book from. Does this look anything like your solution?

Figure 8-3 shows my solution to this problem. My assumption is that the simplest possible solution to this problem is the best solution. And if I must make a few small business process compromises, that is a worthwhile tradeoff.

In my solution (Figure 8-3), when a library purchases a new book, it lets the agency know about the purchase. This much is like the previous solution, but that is where the similarities end.

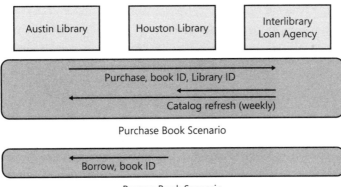

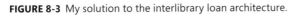

Purchase Book Scenario

Borrow Book Scenario

FIGURE 8-3 My solution to the interlibrary loan architecture.

In my solution, the agency sends out a periodic catalog containing information about which libraries own which books. I have suggested that this catalog be sent out weekly, but this is arbitrary. Then, when Houston wants to borrow a book, it looks up that book in its catalog, finds a library that owns it, and issues a borrow request to that library. In the rare case in which the book is out of stock, the lending library can send a message stating that fact to the borrowing library and the borrowing library can try another library, again based on the information in its catalog.

Which solution is simpler, Figure 8-2 or Figure 8-3? Certainly, if we consider the book-borrowing scenario (by far the most frequent scenario), Figure 8-3 is much simpler. The simple solution requires one single message being sent from the borrowing library to the lending library. In the complex solution, this requires five messages. In the rare case when the book is out of stock at the lending library, the lending library can notify the borrowing library and the borrowing library can try again with some other library.

So we have reduced the typical number of messages required to borrow a book from five to one. Anything else?

It turns out that the simple architecture has many other advantages over the complex architecture. Let's consider the problem of implementing the Interlibrary Loan Agency.

The complex solution requires a complex agency implementation. Consider availability. In the complex solution, the agency is a single point of failure. If the agency goes down, nobody can borrow books. This means that the agency must be implemented using high-availability hardware systems. These systems are expensive and difficult to administer. The simple solution does not need a high-availability solution. If the agency goes down, the only thing affected is the library's ability to update the agency with new purchases. These are not time-critical tasks. If the purchasing library has to wait a day or two to let the agency know about new purchases, who cares?

Let's consider performance. In the complex solution, the agency is the bottleneck. If it falls behind in processing loan requests, the whole system bogs down. This means it must be built not only on highly reliable systems, but on high-performance systems. High-performance systems, like high-availability systems, are expensive and difficult to administer. In the simple solution, the agency just sends out weekly catalog refreshes—that is, one catalog to each library, once a week or so. This is a low workload.

Let's consider the problem of scalability. The scalability of the complex solution is limited by the number of loan requests the agency can handle in a given time. The simple solution has no scalability limitations. It can handle a virtually unlimited number of loan requests.

The bottom line is that complexity affects every aspect of the solution. The complex solution requires complex hardware, database systems, and communications infrastructures. It will require person-years of programming by highly trained personnel, and it will be expensive to maintain and update. The simple solution can be implemented on a cheap PC running over the Internet, and it can be programmed in a few weeks by one programmer using Microsoft Visual Basic. Updates will be trivial, and maintenance will be cheap.

As you can see, complexity is not just a problem for the CIO or the enterprise architect. Complexity has an impact on every aspect of IT systems—from cost to scalability and from performance to reliability. Complexity affects everything and everybody.

A Philosophy of Simplicity

We frequently hear that IT systems are getting more complex, as if this is a natural consequence of living in the 21st century. In reality, however, it is not *systems* that are getting more complex but *system requirements* that are getting more complex. It is not the job of the enterprise architect to design ever more complex systems. It is the job of the enterprise architect to design simple systems that do complex things. It is the job of the enterprise architect to resist the temptation to build complex systems. And it is the job of the CIO to hold the enterprise architect accountable to this goal.

A famous letter attributed to various writers started with this disclaimer: "I'm sorry this letter is so long. I didn't have time to write a short letter." I can imagine enterprise architects giving a similar disclaimer: "I'm sorry this architecture is so complicated. I didn't have time to make it simple."

The paradox about complexity is that it is simple to make systems complex; it is complex to make systems simple. Many people think that it takes a lot of talent to create a highly complicated architecture. That isn't true. It takes a lot of talent to take complicated ideas and realize them in a simple architecture.

Anybody can create a complex architecture. It takes no skill at all. Architectures naturally seek the maximum possible level of complexity all on their own. If it is a complex architecture you are after, you don't even need architects. You might as well just fire them all and let the developers work on their own.

This observation that architectures are naturally attracted to complexity is actually predicted by physics—in particular, the law of entropy. This fundamental law of physics states that left to their own, all systems evolve to a state of maximal disorder (entropy). It takes a constant inflow of energy into a system to keep the disorder at bay. In this regard, enterprise architectures are just another natural system, like gas molecules in a balloon.

The law of entropy tells us that the battle for simplicity is never over. It requires a constant influx of energy to keep enterprise systems simple. It isn't enough to design them so that they are simple. It isn't enough to even build them so that they are simple. You must continue working to prevent an erosion of simplicity for the life of the system. In this sense, the work of the enterprise architect is never done.

The enterprise architect should have a passion for simplicity. People without this passion can be developers, even solution architects. But they cannot be enterprise architects. They are far too dangerous in this role.

A Review of the Book Content

This book describes the various tools that the enterprise architect needs to control complexity. These tools include a mathematical model for complexity and a process for removing complexity from systems. Both the model and the process can be adapted for understanding and controlling complexity in many types of systems, but in this book we have looked specifically at how this model and process apply to enterprise architectures.

The basic model of complexity that I have described states that complexity is related to the number of states in which a system can find itself or the number of paths a system can take. Actually, both the number of states and the number of paths are closely related.

One can calculate these numbers using probability theory. Although you can't measure the complexity of a system directly using this approach, you can compare the relative complexity of two different systems.

After you have used probability theory to calculate relative complexity, you can use partition theory to show how to reduce complexity. The basic approach to complexity control is to partition functionality so that it is separated into autonomous units. These units are called, in an enterprise architecture, *autonomous business capabilities* (ABCs). After you have identified these units, you can take further steps to simplify them by removing extraneous functionality, consolidating redundant functionality, and delegating noncritical functionality.

At the end of this process, you end up with a collection of ABCs that must be implemented. At this point, you shift gears to iteration. First you prioritize the order in which you will implement these ABCs based on risk and value. Then you iterate through them.

The partitioning stage divides the enterprise into manageable subsets. The simplification stage minimizes the complexity of these subsets. The prioritization stage determines the optimal order of delivery. And the iteration stage implements the desired architecture one ABC at a time.

I call this process SIP. SIP stands for *simple iterative partitions*. SIP is the process for reducing complexity in enterprise architectures. It is not an all-encompassing process for creating enterprise architectures. Instead, it seeks to plug the hole in existing methodologies, giving them a way of addressing the one issue they otherwise have no way to address: complexity.

A Parting Message

All enterprise architectural methodologies (including SIP) must ultimately be judged on how well they deliver business value. As I said in my initial definition of *enterprise architecture,*

> *An enterprise architecture is a description of the goals of an organization, how these goals are realized by business processes, and how these business processes can be better served through technology.*

Most methodologies try to build an enterprise architecture by first architecting the business systems and then architecting technology systems to support those business processes. Without an approach to managing complexity, however, the resulting architectures can end up quite convoluted, as shown in Figure 8-4.

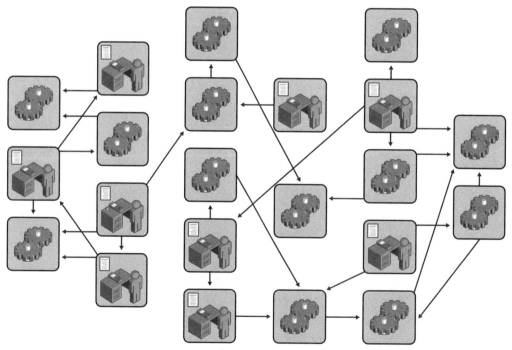

FIGURE 8-4 Typical enterprise architecture.

The SIP enterprise architecture is much more manageable, as shown in Figure 8-5.

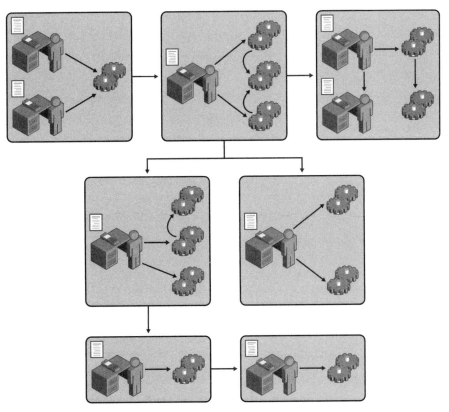

FIGURE 8-5 Typical SIP enterprise architecture.

Simplicity is not free. It takes dedication, discipline, and experience to architect for simplicity. But the resulting architectures are *much* easier to implement, *much* easier to maintain, and *much* more likely to deliver value. Which system do you think is more likely to be delivering business value not only today, but five years down the line—the typical system shown in Figure 8-4 or the simple SIP system shown in Figure 8-5?

The answer is simple. The answer is SIP.

Appendix
This Book at a Glance

This appendix provides brief explanations of key concepts discussed in the book and provides a single location where most of the important concepts can easily be found for review. The appendix divides these concepts into the following three sections, which mirror the overall structure of the book:

- Mathematical Concepts
- Enterprise Architecture Concepts
- SIP Concepts

This arrangement provides a context for the concepts as you review them.

Mathematical Concepts

SIP is based on a mathematical model for complexity and how partitioning reduces complexity. It is not necessary to understand this model fully to use SIP, but it helps and, for many, makes the reasons for the process more understandable.

Mathematical Definition of a Partition

A partition is a set of subsets that divide up some universe such that every element in the original universe ends up in one and only one of the subsets.

Five Laws of Partitions

The Five Laws of Partitions are as follows:

- **First Law of Partitions**   Partitions must be true partitions in the mathematical sense. For an enterprise architecture, this means that the enterprise must be broken up into a set of subsets such that every function in the enterprise ends up residing in one and only one of the subsets. In simple iterative partitions (SIP), these subsets are called ABCs (autonomous business capabilities).

- **Second Law of Partitions**   Partition definitions must be appropriate to the problem at hand. For an enterprise architecture, this means that ABCs must contain functions that are closely related to each other. For all practical purposes, this means that functionality must be assigned to ABCs based on the equivalence relation synergistic.

- **Third Law of Partitions**   The numbers of subsets in a partition must be appropriate. For an enterprise architecture, this means that the number of ABCs that make up a given partition should be in the range of 3 through 10.

- **Fourth Law of Partitions**   The size of the subsets in a partition must be roughly equal. For an enterprise architecture, this means that you don't want to end up with large disparities between the amount of functionality in the different ABCs of the partition.

- **Fifth Law of Partitions**   The interactions between subsets in the partitions must be minimal and well defined. In an enterprise architecture, this means that interactions between different ABCs must be tightly regulated. In practice, this means that you should use the software fortress model to define how software systems interact.

Measuring States in a System of Dice-Like Systems

In any system of dice-like entities, the number of possible states (S) of the system as a whole is related to the number of dice (D) in the system and the number of faces (F) of each of the dice in the following way:

$S = F^D$

When those dice are partitioned into subsets, the number of possible states (S) of the system as a whole is related to the number of dice (D) in each subset, the number of faces (F) of those dice, and the number of subsets in the partition (P) in the following way:

$S = F^D \times P$

Homomorphism

Two systems—say, A and B—are said to be homomorphic when some relationship exists between A and B such that predictions can be made about one system by observing outcomes in the other. In this book, business processes and software systems are shown to have a homomorphic relation with systems of dice-like entities with respect to system complexity.

Equivalence Relations

Any function (F) is defined to be an equivalence relation when the following five properties are all true for any elements a, b, and c of some universe:

- F takes exactly two arguments. In other words, F is a binary function.

- F (a, b) is either True or False. In other words, F is a Boolean function.

- F (a, a) is always True. In other words, F is a reflexive function.

- If F (a, b) is True, then F (b, a) is True. In other words, F is a symmetric function.

- If F (a, b) is True and F (b, c) is True, then F (a, c) is True. In other words, F is a transitive function.

Inverse Equivalence Relations

A function (~F) is an inverse equivalence relation if the following properties are all true for any elements a and b of some universe:

- There exists some function F such that F is shown to be an equivalence relation for that universe.

- Whenever F (a, b) is True, then ~F (a, b) is False.

- Whenever F (a, b) is False, then ~F (a, b) is True.

Partitions

If F is an equivalence relation and ~F is its inverse equivalence relation and P is a partition created with F, then the following statements will always be true:

- If a and b are members of the same partitioning subset, then F (a, b) will always be True and ~F (a, b) will always be False.

- If a and b are members of two different partitioning subsets, then F (a, b) will always be False and ~F (a, b) will always be True.

Partitioning Algorithm for Equivalence Relations

Any equivalence relation (E) can be used to partition a universe. The algorithm is as follows:

1. Pick one of the elements that has not yet been assigned a subset. Let's call this element E1.

2. Choose one of the subsets from the set of subsets. Let's call this subset S1.

3. Choose one random element from S1. Let's call this R1.

4. Check E (E1, R1).

5. If the result is TRUE, then assign E1 to S1.

6. If the result is FALSE, then start again at step 2 with another subset.

7. If you exhaust all the subsets without finding a home for E1, then create a new subset and assign E1 to that new subset.

8. Continue with step 1 until all the unassigned elements have been exhausted.

Enterprise Architectural Concepts

Although SIP can be used to simplify both business processes and software systems in isolation, the biggest bang for the buck from a complexity perspective comes when SIP is used at a level that encompasses both business processes and software systems. This is the level of enterprise architecture.

Preferred Definition of Enterprise Architecture

An enterprise architecture is a description of the goals of an organization, how these goals are realized by business processes, and how these business processes can be better served through technology.

Definition of Optimal Architecture

An optimal architecture is one that is as simple as possible. In practice, this means an architecture that has been optimally partitioned—that is, partitioned in such a way that any further partitioning would actually increase complexity due to lack of autonomy.

Boyd's Law of Iteration

Boyd's Law of Iteration states the following: In implementing complex systems, it is better to act quickly (and iteratively) rather than perfectly (and in a big-bang fashion).

Laws of Enterprise Complexity

A software system is, from a complexity perspective, a dice-like system in which variables behave like dice and states of those variables behave like face on the dice.

A business process is, from a complexity perspective, a dice-like system in which decision points behave like dice and the numbers of emanating paths from the decision points behave like face on the dice.

The following laws describe how these variables, states, paths, and decision points are related to complexity in their related systems:

- **Sessions' Law of Software Complexity**   The complexity of a software system is a function of the number of states in which that system can find itself.

- **Sessions' First Corollary of Software Complexity**   The relative complexity of two software systems—say, system A and system B—is the same as the ratio of the number of states in which A can find itself divided by the number of states in which B can find itself.

- **Sessions' Law of Business Process Complexity**   The complexity of a business process is a function of the number of paths possible in the process.

- **Sessions' First Corollary of Business Process Complexity**   The relative complexity of two business processes—say, system A and system B—is equal to the number of paths of process A divided by the number of states of process B.

Synergistic and Autonomous

The function Synergistic S is defined over a universe of enterprise functionality such that for any two elements of functionality (a and b), S (a, b) is True if the function a always requires the function b and the function b always requires the function a.

The function Autonomous A is defined over a universe of enterprise functionality such that for any two elements of functionality (a and b), A (a, b) is True if the function a does not always require the function b or the function b does not always require the function a.

Given these definitions, synergistic is an *equivalence relation* and autonomous is its *inverse equivalence relation*.

SIP Concepts

SIP is the methodology this book proposes to control the complexity of enterprise architectures. Controlling the complexity of these architectures is critical to an organization's ability to realize business value from its IT investments.

Definition of SIP

SIP stands for *simple iterative partitions*. It is a process by which an enterprise is partitioned into autonomous subsets called ABCs (autonomous business capabilities). Those ABCs are then simplified using any of several simplification algorithms. Finally, the ABCs are iteratively delivered.

The SIP Process

The main goals of the simple iterative partitions (SIP) process are as follows:

- **Complexity Control**   No surprise here. Reducing complexity is the focal point.

- **Logic-Based Decisions**   Most enterprise architecture decisions are based on instinct, gut feeling, politics, vendor loyalty, and so on. SIP seeks to remove these emotion-based (irrational) decisions and instead approach every decision from a rational and mathematically grounded perspective.

- **Value-Driven Deliverables**   SIP is value-driven. All deliverables are measured against quantifiable business value.

- **Reproducible Results**   SIP provides a methodology that is reproducible. Two SIP practitioners analyzing a similar enterprise should come up with architectural solutions that are similar.

- **Verifiable Architectures**   SIP produces architectures that can be mathematically verified.

- **Flexible Methodology**   SIP can be used with most other enterprise architecture methodologies because SIP completes them by addressing concerns that the other methodologies do not address.

Figure A-1 shows the SIP process at a glance.

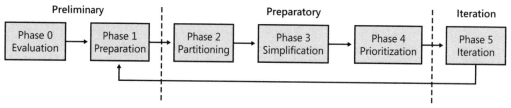

FIGURE A-1 The SIP process.

Here are the phase descriptions for the phases shown in the preceding figure:

- **Phase 0: Evaluation**   Evaluate the need for an enterprise architecture in general and SIP in particular.

- **Phase 1: Preparation**   Train in the importance of complexity control and the enterprise methodology.

- **Phase 2: Partitioning**   Partition enterprise functionality into autonomous business capabilities (ABCs).

- **Phase 3: Simplification**   Conduct simplification of enterprise architecture by removal of unnecessary functionality and consolidation or removal of ABCs.

- **Phase 4: Prioritization**   Determine priority order of ABC delivery based on business value, technical risk, and other factors.

- **Phase 5: Iteration**   Perform iterative delivery of ABCs based on priority order.

ABC

ABC stands for *autonomous business capability*. An ABC contains both the business processes and software systems that are in a synergistic relationship to each other. The collection of ABCs constitutes a partition of the enterprise.

Software Fortress Model

The basic software fortress model is shown in Figure A-2. Remember that a software fortress is essentially the technical component inside an ABC.

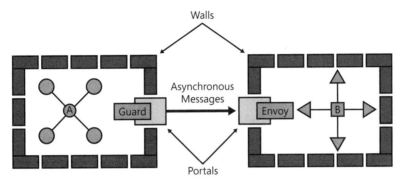

FIGURE A-2 Basic software fortress model.

The main rules governing software fortresses are as follows:

- **Rule 1: Autonomy**   The software systems inside a fortress are autonomous with respect to systems outside the fortress.

- **Rule 2: Explicit Boundaries**   You always know when you are inside or outside a fortress.

- **Rule 3: Partitioning of Functionality**   An enterprise's collection of technical services is partitioned by the software fortresses.

- **Rule 4: Dependencies Defined by Policy**   Any dependencies between fortresses are defined by policies. Policies describe only the messages that pass between fortresses.

- **Rule 5: Asynchronicity**   All (or at least, most) communications between fortresses take place asynchronously.

- **Rule 6: Partitioning of Data**   The technical partition defined by the software fortresses extends through the data.

- **Rule 7: No Cross-Fortress Transactions**   Database-style transactions must never cross a fortress boundary.

- **Rule 8: Single-Point Security**   The guard is the single point of security.

- **Rule 9: Inside Trust**   Software systems (including the data storage system) trust all systems that are inside the fortress boundaries.

- **Rule 10: Keep It Simple**   Do not put in place fortress policies that are not driven by documented enterprise need.

Three Styles of ABC Communications

Partner relationships between ABCs—say A and B—are almost entirely driven by three styles of communications. They are as follows:

- **Information Request**   Partner A needs some information that it knows Partner B has and asks for it.

- **Information Broadcast**   Partner A has some information that it knows Partner B (and perhaps others) would like to know, so it delivers it.

- **Work Request**   Partner A would like Partner B to execute some work on its behalf.

The SIP Mantra

The SIP mantra is the summary of the entire SIP philosophy. It should be repeated over and over by everybody involved in enterprise architectures, business processes, or IT systems. It should be the motto stitched on every shirt, the banner hung from every hall, the common pledge recited at the start of every meeting. It is this:

"Complexity Is The Enemy"

Index

Author Biography

Roger Sessions is the CTO of ObjectWatch. He has written seven books, including *Software Fortresses: Modeling Enterprise Architectures,* and more than 100 articles. He is on the Board of Directors of the International Association of Software Architects, is Editor-in-Chief of *Perspectives* of the International Association of Software Architects, and is a Microsoft recognized MVP in enterprise architecture. He has given talks in more than 30 countries and 70 cities, and at 100 conferences on the topic of enterprise architecture. He consults with major corporations and public-sector organizations throughout the world on the need to understand, model, and control complexity at the enterprise architectural level. *ComputerWorld* (New Zealand) describes him as "The Simplicity Guru." He holds multiple patents in software engineering and enterprise architecture.

More than 10,000 developers, architects, and executives follow Roger's writing regularly in his *ObjectWatch Newsletter*, now in its fifteenth year. For a free subscription or for information on contacting Roger, see the *ObjectWatch* web site at *www.objectwatch.com.*

ObjectWatch offers the SIP methodology for controlling enterprise architectural complexity primarily through partner relationships. For information about a SIP partner in your area, or to inquire about becoming a SIP partner, contact *information@objectwatch.com.*

What do you think of this book?

We want to hear from you!

Do you have a few minutes to participate in a brief online survey?

Microsoft is interested in hearing your feedback so we can continually improve our books and learning resources for you.

To participate in our survey, please visit:

www.microsoft.com/learning/booksurvey/

...and enter this book's ISBN-10 or ISBN-13 number (located above barcode on back cover*). As a thank-you to survey participants in the United States and Canada, each month we'll randomly select five respondents to win one of five $100 gift certificates from a leading online merchant. At the conclusion of the survey, you can enter the drawing by providing your e-mail address, which will be used for prize notification only.

Thanks in advance for your input. Your opinion counts!

* Where to find the ISBN on back cover

ISBN-13: 000-0-0000-0000-0
ISBN-10: 0-0000-0000-0

Example only. Each book has unique ISBN.

Microsoft®
Press

No purchase necessary. Void where prohibited. Open only to residents of the 50 United States (includes District of Columbia) and Canada (void in Quebec). For official rules and entry dates see:

www.microsoft.com/learning/booksurvey/